W9-BUC-154

Under Saturn's Shadow

Marie-Louise von Franz, Honorary Patron

**Studies in Jungian Psychology
by Jungian Analysts**

Daryl Sharp, General Editor

UNDER SATURN'S SHADOW

The Wounding and Healing of Men

James Hollis

For Dad, for brother Alan,
for son Timothy, son Jonah, son-in-law Daniel
and for daughter Taryn

Canadian Cataloguing in Publication Data

Hollis, James, 1936-
    Under Saturn's shadow: the wounding and healing of men

(Studies in Jungian psychology by Jungian analysts; 63)

Includes bibliographical references and index.

ISBN 0-919123-64-3

1. Fear.
2. Psychoanalysis.
3. Jung, C.G. (Carl Gustav), 1875-1961.
I. Title.   II. Series.

BF575.55.F2H65 1994   152.4'6   C94-930192-2

Copyright © 1994 by James Hollis.
All rights reserved.

INNER CITY BOOKS
Box 1271, Station Q, Toronto, Canada M4T 2P4
Telephone (416) 927-0355
FAX (416) 924-1814

Honorary Patron: Marie-Louise von Franz.
Publisher and General Editor: Daryl Sharp.
Senior Editor: Victoria Cowan.

INNER CITY BOOKS was founded in 1980 to promote the
understanding and practical application of the work of C.G. Jung.

Cover: "They Offered Him the Crown of Stars," collage,
10 1/2" x 13 1/2". Copyright © 1993 by Rick Jones.

Printed and bound in Canada by
University of Toronto Press Incorporated

CONTENTS

See final page for descriptions of other Inner City Books

Remember, you've come here having already
understood the necessity of struggling with yourself,
only with yourself. Therefore, thank everyone
who gives you the opportunity.
—Gurdjieff, *Meetings with Remarkable Men.*

Introduction

This book derives from a talk given at the Philadelphia Jung Center in April 1992. That talk was long overdue. I had personally avoided the topic for a decade even though men's suffering, aspirations and healing had progressively occupied my time as a Jungian analyst. Twelve years ago, the ratio of women to men analysands in my practice was nine to one. Currently I see more men by a ratio of six to four. I believe this shift is replicated in the offices of other therapists, and the reasons for it have also contributed to the rise of the men's movement. I avoided the topic because so much seemed in flux. At best I saw a massive work of scholarship and emotional cleansing, at worst a pop-psych phenomenon I found distasteful.

I am very much concerned with the healing and transformation of individuals. This work is usually so intense, so deeply personal, that it is often easy to forget the larger world and the vast social problems of which we are all a part and through which we are all wounded. But it became increasingly clear to me that the stories of individual men did overlap and present consistent motifs. As women have learned before us, I began to realize that the collective experience of men is an inescapable part of their personal history as well. The warp and woof of private history and public mythology meld into the formation of individual character.

By now, of course, there are many fine books on various aspects of the dilemma of modern men. In this book I shall draw from them at times, directly, consciously and gratefully. We are all part of the struggle toward community and each of our voices has a different ring. I do not aim to offer an original contribution to men's scholarship, but rather to take complex matters and distill them, integrate them and express them in terms that can be apprehended by many. Similarly, I draw upon the clinical experience of men in therapy. To them, also, I am grateful for permission to use their material.

The purpose of *Under Saturn's shadow,* then, is to offer a synoptic view of men's wounding and healing, and to examine where things stand in this last decade of the century.

But, even more, a sort of confession—I avoided speaking out on this subject for many years, not only because the issues seemed so much in transition, but because I too have suffered from living under the shadow of Saturn and am not always clear about where I stand in relationship to my own masculine nature. Fate had it that I be born into the male gender. For many years I simply took that accident and its consequences for granted and believed it more frightening than liberating to try to step out from under the shadow. In the pages that follow, I shall cite autobiographical examples from time to time, not to indulge myself but because I think them typical and representative. As the painter Tony Berlant observed, "The more personal and introspective a work of art is, the more universal it becomes."[1]

In focusing on men's issues, it is not my intention to minimize the wounds of women. We of the male gender owe a deep debt of gratitude to those women who have spoken out, not only to express their own pain within our sexist culture, but also to free men to be more fully themselves. Their *cri de coeur* has helped men look more consciously to their own wounding, and we are all better served as a result. The example of women struggling to free themselves from the shadows of the collective gives courage and makes it necessary for men to do likewise. Unless men can emerge from darkness, we shall continue to wound women and each other, and the world can never be a safe or healthy place. This work we do, then, is not only for ourselves but also for those around us.

In the middle of the last century the Danish theologian Soren Kierkegaard observed that one could not save one's age, only express the conviction that it was perishing.[2] The unconscious forces, the public institutions and ideologies that guide our lives, have such inertial momentum that one cannot hope to bring rapid change to society and its gender roles. However, the first requisite is that men be-

---

[1] Peter Clothier, "Hammering Out Magic," in *Art News,* p. 113.
[2] *The Journals of Kierkegaard,* p. 165.

come conscious of the fact that they are grievously wounded. The unconsciousness of their trauma causes them to repeatedly wound themselves and women as well. I often puzzle over how women could not but grow to hate men who oppress them, and almost equally how men grow to hate and fear each other.

This, then, is a book that draws on the work of many in order to bring individual men to greater awareness and to further the dialogue that must transpire for healing. The imagos consciously and unconsciously governing our lives can only be worked through in private, individual suffering, but the growing ability of men to confess their grief and rage, to participate in a growing conversation with each other, will also help to heal the world's wound.

I invite the reader to see him- or herself in the journey described here. For women, the description of the struggle with the mother complex, for example, may be useful in understanding that strange ambivalence which seems to afflict the men in their lives. The masculine journey has many passages, many perils. The rigors and tasks we can identify are those we are most likely to experience meaningfully. It is not true that what we do not know will not hurt us; indeed, what we do not know hurts us deeply and, like Samson, we may then blindly pull the temple down upon our own heads.

To bring each of us to greater consciousness of male transits and torments, I am obliged to tell male secrets. I reveal them so that women might better understand. Some of these secrets may be new to men themselves, though I seriously doubt that a single male reader of this book will disagree that they point to wounds he has carried in his own isolated and frightened heart. If we may not end the wounding, and the fear, we may at least end the isolation.

*

The title of this book alludes to the fact that men, as well as women, labor always under the heavy shadow of ideologies, some conscious, some inherited from family and ethnic group, some part of the fabric of a nation's history and its mythic soil. This shadow is an oppressive weight on the soul. Men labor under it, oppressed and blighted in spirit. The experience of this weighty shadow is saturnine. The definitions of what it means to be a man—male roles and expectations, competition and animosity, the shaming and devaluing of many of men's better qualities and capacities—all lead to the crushing weight. This burden has always been there, but today men of courage are beginning to question the necessity of living under it.

Saturn was the Roman god of agriculture. On the one hand, as a god of generativity, he helped create early Roman civilization; on the other hand he was associated with a string of dark and bloody stories. His earlier, Greek incarnation, Cronus, was born of the male principle Uranus and the female principle Ge or Gaia. Uranus hated his children for he feared their potential; legend tells us he was "the first to devise shameful actions."[3] His wife Gaia fashioned a sickle and induced Cronus to attack his father. Cronus struck and severed his father's phallus. From the drops of blood that fell on the earth were born fearsome giants. The sperm-flecked, fecundated sea gave birth to Aphrodite, whose name means "born of the foam."[4]

Cronus-Saturn replaced his father and became a tyrant of equal magnitude. Whenever he and his consort Rhea produced children, he ate them. The only child who evaded this fate was Zeus. In turn, Zeus led a revolt against the father and a ten-year war ensued. With Zeus's triumph many civilizing forces emerged, but he, too, fell prey to the power complex and became tyrannical.[5]

Thus the Cronus-Saturn story is one of power, jealousy, insecurity—violence to the principle of eros, to generativity and to the earth. As Jung once noted, where power is, love is not.[6] Along with the great capacity for empowerment that the gods dramatize, we see its corruption in the power complex. Power in itself is neutral, but

---

[3] *Crowell's Handbook of Classical Literature,* p. 109.

[4] Ibid., p. 41.

[5] His oppression of Prometheus and others is well known. See, for instance, Edith Hamilton, *Mythology,* pp. 75-78.

[6] "Where love reigns, there is no will to power; and where the will to power is paramount, love is lacking." ("The Problem of the Attitude-Type," *Two Essays on Analytical Psychology,* CW 7, par. 78) [CW refers to *The Collected Works of C.G. Jung*]

without eros it is haunted by fear and compensatory ambition, driven to violent ends. As Shakespeare observed, "Uneasy lies the head that wears a crown."[7]

Most men through history have grown up under the shadow of this Saturnian legacy. They have suffered from the corruption of empowerment, driven by fear, wounding themselves and others. Modern men may feel there are no alternatives, that Saturn's legacy is the only game in town. I don't believe it is.

Under Saturn's Shadow is offered to the reader in order to identify some of the many ways in which this dark mythos has scarred our souls. My hope is that it might move each person to look within and to seek greater personal freedom.

The Eight Secrets Men Carry Within

1. Men's lives are as much governed by restrictive role expectations as are the lives of women.
2. Men's lives are essentially governed by fear.
3. The power of the feminine is immense in the psychic economy of men.
4. Men collude in a conspiracy of silence whose aim is to suppress their emotional truth.
5. Because men must leave Mother, and transcend the mother complex, wounding is necessary.
6. Men's lives are violent because their souls have been violated.
7. Every man carries a deep longing for his father and for his tribal Fathers.
8. If men are to heal, they must activate within what they did not receive from without.

---

[7] *Henry IV,* part 2, scene 3, line 31.

1

The Saturnian Legacy:
Tapes, Roles, Expectations

"Man is born free, and everywhere he is in chains." Thus began Jean Jacques Rousseau's *The Social Contract, or Principles of Political Right,* in 1762. We all are born free, bearing the germ of wholeness and health, and then life happens. Since children are dependent upon their parents and their culture for the fulfillment of basic needs, they are quickly estranged from that natural being. We are all socialized to serve and maintain the collective, family structures and social institutions that have a life of their own but require the repeated sacrifice of the individual to sustain them.

In the texture of our bones, in the fabric of our nerves, in the corridors of memory, we carry that precious child still. Who of us, like the young James Agee, did not lie out on the grass, under the stars of a summer night, and wonder at the mystery of it all, the child intuiting the large questions before it? "We are talking now of summer evenings in Knoxville, Tennessee, in the time that I lived there so successfully disguised to myself as a child."[8] As the big folk came out after dinner, adjusted the bell spray of the sprinkler, rocked on the creaking porch swing, the child we were drifted off into reverie until,

> Sleep, soft smiling, draws me unto her: and those receive me, who quietly treat me, as one familiar and well-beloved in that home: but will not, oh, will not, not now, not ever; but will not ever tell me who I am.[9]

Agee's remembrance of things past is replicated in the lives of each of us—the wonder of being on this spinning earth, the vague

---

[8] *A Death in the Family,* p. 11.
[9] Ibid., p. 15.

angst-laden mists that hover about the path into the future and still the joy of life coursing through our veins. And where did it go? Why the heaviness, the body ache, the soul fatigue, the ennui of brain and bone? What happened to that child, afraid but full of itself? He lives still in moments of spontaneity, in "a lonely impulse of delight,"[10] and in the gossamer dreams that slip from awareness as we head off to work. He lives still, but very deep within, and he is weary and heavily laden with the Saturnian shadow.

Let me illustrate with a personal example. Once in awhile my father would laugh, or make a joke, or even whistle. Even as a child I came to realize that when he whistled things were very dark indeed; however, even then, I recognized an heroic impulse on his part. To invoke the cliché, he was whistling in the dark. After awhile I began to realize that when he whistled it was not joy time but dark time. All his good efforts notwithstanding, I knew things were difficult.

My father had had to end his formal education in the eighth grade because his father had lost his business in agricultural equipment due to the Great Depression and the failure of the farms that hit the Midwest even before the crash of '29. The clear message to my father, to which he responded then and for the rest of his life, was that he had to sacrifice his own interests and work to support his people.

Later, when I entered the picture as the elder child, he worked all day at Allis-Chalmers on the assembly line building tractors and earth-moving equipment, and on nights and weekends he drove a truck and shoveled coal into people's homes. In later years he was promoted, ironically, to the position of "analyst" on the assembly line, with the power to tell college-educated engineers where they had screwed up. In his years there he had learned the whole system. He could analyze the problems and became a trouble-shooter.

For fifty years he showed up every Friday with his paycheck that paid, or almost paid, the bills outstanding. We never went hungry, as my best friend Kent sometimes did, but I knew even then that my

---

[10] W.B. Yeats, "An Irish Airman Foresees His Death," line 11, in *The Collected Poems of W.B. Yeats.*

father worried that we would. And I also received my first Saturnian message from him, clearly and irrevocably, that to be a man meant to work. It meant to work always, any work which supported those for whom one was responsible. It meant that personal satisfaction was set aside before fidelity to that enormous responsibility. Years later, when a woman asked me what I wanted inscribed on my tombstone, I said, "Here lies one who could be counted upon." So powerful was this injunction that my father, and later I, was prepared to die for it, and to be memorialized for it.

Years later, when I wrote a note to my father on his birthday card, he responded across the gulf between us: "I am sorry I didn't get to know you boys so well because I was always working." He was taking on the blame for us growing and developing apart, even as I honored him for his fidelity and service to us. I knew he was serving us, suffering for us, worrying on our behalf, and I never once thought ill of him for his work. But I also knew that it did not serve him. Even then I knew: it did not serve him, but apparently that was what it meant to be a man.

During these same formative years World War Two was unfolding. I saw the big folk gathered anxiously around the radio to hear of battles raging in Europe and the South Pacific, and to think on loved ones who were in such strange places as Tulagi, Mindanao and the ball-turret of a B-17 tail gunner. (All of them did come back; the twenty-four year old returned from the Philippines with his hair totally white and the tail gunner with a piece of flak in his leg.)

The black-out curtains, tearful good-byes in train stations, the obvious anxiety, contributed to my sense of something large and awful transpiring, something in which we were all caught up. I also overheard them whispering atrocity stories, such as the one about the family who received a postcard from their son delivered by the International Red Cross. Under the stamp was written, "They cut my tongue out." Whether such stories were always true or not, the adults around me believed they were. That was enough for me.

This constituted my second irrefutable message about being a man. I firmly believed that my fate, apart from being an economic animal, was to grow up and become a soldier, to go to some foreign place and kill or be killed, or come home tortured and maimed. I lay awake nights imagining my fated appointment with such horrors. Just as all of the big people who lived through the Great Depression were irrevocably scarred and apprehensive, so, too, anyone who recalls war times shudders in recollecting the horror and the uncertainty. As a child in the Midwest I was as far from the slaughtered cities as one could imagine, but the combat zones were everywhere and we all were afraid. I had not even heard of such places as Dachau, Bergen-Belsen and Mauthausen then, but when I was an adult I visited them with my children. It was not all paranoia; there was something to worry about and as a man I was expected to be responsive and responsible. Such were the heaviest of the tapes of Saturn, then, the three "W's" one might say: work, war and worry.

All men will recall similar experiences. Each will be able to relate incidents where he felt called to something larger than his capacity to comprehend. Pulled ineluctably into the maelstrom, the child desperately hopes for information, for modeling, for leadership, for instruction, for help in coping with that which will shortly confront and perhaps overwhelm him. If one is to undertake such trials, the youth desperately hopes that "they" will take him aside and teach him what he needs to know.

I recall once glimpsing such mysteries as I felt I needed in order to survive as a man. My father caught a fishhook in the palm of his hand and without expression of any kind pulled it out. I surmised that perhaps the big folk did not feel pain as we little folk did, but I rather suspected he had been taught that mysterious courage I so desperately needed. Perhaps it was not too much to hope that some day "they" would take me aside and teach me how to be a man. I guessed that it might occur when one went to high school. Without knowing about something called puberty, I could see that the folks in high school had bigger bodies than we, that they seemed on the adult side of the great gulf. But, to my surprise, and a disappointment I feel to this day, "they" never took me aside and told me what it means to be a man or how to conduct myself as an adult.

Today, of course, I know that "they," the tribal elders of our time, did not know what it means to be a man either. They similarly were uninitiated and could hardly pass on the mysteries and liberating knowledge they themselves lacked.

In my own halting fashion, I had tumbled to the necessity of rites of passage from childhood to manhood. Not only are such rites about transition from the dependencies of infancy to the self-sufficiency of adulthood, but equally about the transmission of such values as the quality and character of citizenship, and those attitudes and beliefs that connect a person to his gods, to his society and to himself. Yet such rites of passage withered and passed away long ago. "It has often been said," notes Mircea Eliade, "that one of the characteristics of the modern world is the disappearance of any meaningful rites of initiation."[11] Even the phrase "rite of initiation" or "rite of passage" may not be understood in our time.

A *rite* is a movement in and toward depth. Rites are not invented; they are found, discovered, experienced, and they rise out of some archetypal encounter with depth. The purpose of the symbolic act which the rite enacts is to lead into or back toward that experience of depth. Obviously rites repeated can lose their capacity to point beyond themselves into that depth, and they then become empty and sterile. Yet our need for the depth encounter persists. In "The Symbolic Life," Jung speaks of how important it is for a tribe of Pueblo Indians to see their rituals as instrumental in helping the sun to rise.

> That gives peace, when people feel that they are living the symbolic life, that they are actors in the divine drama. That gives the only meaning to human life; everything else is banal and you can dismiss it. A career, producing of children, are all *maya* compared with that one thing, that your life is meaningful.[12]

Without meaningful rites we sustain the most grievous of wounds to the soul—life without depth. The idea of *passage* is similarly essential, for all passages imply something ending, a death of sorts,

---

[11] *Rites and Symbols of Initiation,* p. ix.
[12] *The Symbolic Life,* CW 18, par. 630.

and something beginning, a birth of sorts. Only death is static; the principle of life is change, and we have many deaths and rebirths to transit if we are to lead meaningful lives.[13] *Initiation* implies entry into something new, something mysterious.

Given the fact that rites of passage have largely disappeared from our culture, it behooves men to reflect as individuals on what those rites offered. For what is not available through our culture we are now obliged to find for ourselves. Despite the variety of cultures, and specific local content, the archetypal stages of such rites of passage were remarkably similar. It seems that our predecessors had intuited the importance of such separations and evolutions of personality, and they collectively grasped that these processes were necessary. The duration, intensity and decisiveness of such rites were in direct proportion to the difficulty of truly leaving childhood and growing up. As few in our culture have managed, psychologically speaking, to separate, to grow up, it may profit us to reflect awhile on the stages of initiatory experience. Again, what is not provided us by our culture is left to us to do as individuals. We cannot avoid the task through ignorance, for otherwise the developmental process, becoming a man, remains undone.

Those patterns of passage may be summarized in six stages. While the content of each stage varied according to local custom, the stages themselves were explicit or implied in the various cultural patterns.

The first stage of passage was *separation*, physical separation from the parents in order to begin the psychological separation. This was never a matter of choice for the boy. Often, in the middle of the night, he would be "kidnapped" from his parents by the gods or the demons, the older men of the tribe who wore masks or painted their faces. These masks moved them from the familiar realm of neighbors or uncles to the status of gods or archetypal forces. The abruptness, even violence, of the separation, was a reminder that no youth would voluntarily relinquish the comforts of the hearth. Its warmth, protec-

---

[13] See my book, *The Middle Passage: From Misery to Meaning in Midlife.*

tion and nourishment create an enormous gravitational pull. To remain by the hearth, literally or figuratively, is to remain a child and to forswear one's potential as an adult.

Accordingly, the second stage of the passage was *death*. The boy would be buried, passed through a dark tunnel, plunged into some literal or symbolic darkness. While the experience would of course be terrifying, what the youth was undergoing was the symbolic death of childhood dependency. He was experientially suffering the loss of the hearth. "You can't go home again." It was the loss of innocence, the loss of the Edenic connectedness of childhood. In "dying," the child "wakes to the farm forever fled from the childless land," as Dylan Thomas expressed it.[14]

If there is death, then, life must follow. So, the third stage was a ceremony of *rebirth*. Sometimes a name change accompanied this rebirth, reinforcing the emergence of a new being. (Christian baptism obviously symbolizes such a death-rebirth motif through its return to the umbilical waters. Roman Catholic confirmation and Jewish *bar* and *bat mitzvahs* are survivors of these historic rites.)

The fourth stage of initiation typically involved the *teachings,* imparting such knowledge as the youth would require in order to function as an adult. The teachings were of three different kinds. Practical skills, such as hunting, fishing, defense and herding were critical, for the nascent man was to help sustain and protect his society. The privileges and responsibilities of adulthood and citizenship were similarly transmitted. And, lastly, there was an introduction to the mysteries, so that the young person might have some sense of spiritual grounding and participation in the transcendent realm. "Who are our gods?" "What sort of society, laws, ethics, spirit gifts, did they bestow?" Locating the person in a mythic context bestowed identity, gave a sense of the greater framework in which he participated, and deepened the soul of the youth.

The fifth stage might be characterized as the *ordeal*. The content of the practices might vary, but the boy was required to suffer a separa-

---

[14] "Fern Hill," in *Collected Poems,* p. 180.

tion from the comforts and protections of the hearth. I will say much more about this later, but what strikes us moderns as gratuitous cruelty was in fact a wise perception that such suffering quickened consciousness. Consciousness only comes from suffering; without some form of suffering—physical, emotional, spiritual—we are content to rest easy in the old dispensation, the old comforts, the old dependencies. The second reason for such suffering, frankly, was to help inure the boy to the actual rigors of life he would experience soon enough. While seeming barbarous to us, such practices as circumcision and ritual scarification not only signaled the sacrifice of the comforts of the flesh and childhood dependencies, but were also a sign of election into the company of initiated adults.

Perhaps most significantly, the ordeal usually involved some form of isolation, a retreat to a sacred space away from the community. The essential part of being an adult means not only that one can no longer turn backward to the protection of others, but that one must learn to draw upon inner resources. No one knows he has them until he is obliged to use them. The natural world is dark and full of strange animals and demons, and the confrontation with one's fear is a moment of decisive significance. Ritual isolation is an introduction to a central truth, that no matter how tribal our social life, we are on the journey alone and must learn to draw strength and solace from within, or we will not achieve adulthood. Often the initiate spent months alone, waiting perhaps for the Great Dream, a communication from the gods as to his true name or proper vocation. He learned to depend on his wits, his courage and his weapons, or he perished.

Upon *return*, the last stage, the boy was an adult.

These rituals of passage were elaborate, wisely so, for they were extensive in direct relationship to the power of the mother complex, namely the enormous pull toward dependency in all of us. Elaborate and powerful emotional experiences are required to overcome this inertial gravity. No one in his right mind would willingly separate, hence lethargy, fear and dependency dominate, or threaten to, the lives of us all. In traditional cultures the rites were more elaborate for boys than for girls, for girls were expected to leave their personal mothers but circle back to the hearth.[15] Again, the rites of separation were decisive and powerful for boys, not only because of the power of the mother complex but because boys were expected to separate from the natural world, the life of instinct, for an artificial, man-made world of culture.

Economics, for example, is a wholly artificial construct. Money, paychecks, stock options—these are concepts upon which much of man's life depends and upon which much of his soul is projected. Food in the mouth or hunger are instinctual experiences; wampum, checks or bonuses are artificial. To separate a child from the instinctual world requires a numinous construct at least as powerful as his urge to settle back into unconsciousness.

The elaborateness of the traditional rites of passage was necessary, then, to bridge the huge gulf between childhood and adulthood, between boyish instinctual life and dependency and the independent self-sufficiency of manhood. If the rites worked, the boy experienced an existential change; he died as one being and became another. But, as we all know, such rites today are missing, such existential transformation driven underground. If we ask a man, "Do you feel like a man?" chances are he will consider the question silly or threatening. He will know his roles, but he will neither be able to define what it means to be a man, nor will he likely feel he has measured up to any of his own partial definitions. In short, the wise elders are gone, lost to death, depression, alcoholism or corporate boardrooms and golden parachutes. The bridge from childhood to manhood is washed out.

As men have no meaningful rites of passage available to them, no wise elders to transmit what lies on the other side, they have necessarily had to take their clues from societal role expectations and essentially hollow role models. All the while, the pain and confusion to the soul is pushed inward, or acted out violently, or distanced from

---

[15] Today the gender expectations for girls have exploded and women are increasingly free to pursue differentiated lives. Thus they too need rites of passage into adulthood. See, for instance, Sylvia Brinton Perera, *Descent to the Goddess: A Way of Initiation for Women.*.

consciousness. Accordingly, the gap between wisdom and experience has been filled in by outer images, images which, as has been true for women as well, seldom feed the soul.

Hence the first of the great secrets to be openly acknowledged is that *men's lives are as much governed by role expectations as are the lives of women.* And the corollary is that those roles do not support, confirm or resonate to the needs of men's souls.

It is the growing awareness of this terrible discrepancy between role expectations and the needs of the soul that has given rise to what is called the men's movement. While no representative institution or body has emerged (such as the National Organization for Women), nor has there evolved a clear socio-political agenda, the scattered men's groups and growing body of literature attest to the stirring of awareness that something is terribly wrong. The need for such a movement is succinctly summarized by John Lee:

> It's an emotional movement, a releasing of the pain and poison men have been holding in their collective stomachs for centuries. It is not power oriented in any way, but powerful in that it frees men and their spirits from the tyranny of the old paradigm of "Don't feel. Die younger than women. Don't talk. Don't grieve. Don't get angry. Don't rock the boat. Don't trust other men. Don't put passion before bill paying. Follow the crowd, not your bliss."[16]

I concur entirely with these sentiments. However, the shadow of power inevitably creeps into any group, any movement. When overly socialized and domesticated, men have rightly felt a longing for something wild and very deep; still, the average man will never join a group, would feel ridiculous meeting out in the forest to beat a drum, and will seldom risk being vulnerable with other men. I do not criticize those who have gone into the forest and wept and raged and beat the drum, for they have frequently found something needed for their souls. At the same time such activity may have as much long-term relevance as bra burning now occupies in the long march of women toward dignity and equal opportunity. Bra burning was an

---

[16] *At My Father's Wedding,* p. xviii.

important emotional release, for a few at least, but to my mind such energies are more effectively spent in discussion, in court and in working toward cultural change.

We are still at an early stage of understanding men's experience and many will have to find a form of emotional release and a way to share their pain with others. But I suspect that future generations will look back on this era of wild man retreats with a sort of bemused nostalgia, even as we think of the communes of the sixties—well intended, but having little impact on the course of history.

Recently I visited my son in Santa Fe where he is living and struggling to be an artist. We drove up into the Jemez Mountains, so far up that the road ran out on us. We saw owls, deer and two very large black birds sitting on a rock. When we got closer we realized that the rock had legs and two predators were munching on a moose. We were far from civilization and we joked that if it suddenly snowed they would also find the bodies of two Anglos in the spring thaw. We returned to the Santa Fe plaza with the warm feeling of having had a primal adventure.

Crossing the street my son saw a leader of the local men's group and introduced me to him. Immediately the man began quizzing me about what I knew, who I knew, if I had drummed, and so on. I felt myself pulled, involuntarily, into a competitive mood. Then, quite nicely, he invited me to attend a name-changing ceremony for two men reaching their fiftieth birthday the next day. When I said I had to fly out of Albuquerque to Atlantic City at 7:30 the next morning, he said, "I'll throw a fast one at you now. Why do you spend so little time with your son?"

I began to say that I had to get back to work to pay the bills, a classic male defense (and also reality), but my son interceded before I had finished, saying, "This is his third visit to see me this year." "Oh, okay," the man said, and we parted.

My son and I reflected on the encounter and noted how, for all the consciousness this man professed to have, he had negatively charged the meeting with male issues. He set me up to feel competitive and I fell for it; then he sought to shame me as a father. He was operating,

I believe, without conscious malice, and I may indeed be guilty of compulsive working and be less than the perfect father, but both of us fell into the trap long prepared for men. Surely it is not the purpose of the men's movement to reinforce these old complexes, to set men against each other, as he unwittingly had.

In this duel at high noon on the plaza in Santa Fe, no six-guns were drawn, but shots were fired and wounds suffered in an exchange that lasted 240 seconds but reached back as far as memory. A man who was a leader of the "movement" had, in welcoming me, fired at me. Sizing me up, his complex was triggered and he set about questioning me in ways that stir old passions, old competitive reflexes. Then, subtly the shadow problem of power insinuated itself, and he sought to shame me as an absent father. His question aimed to set him one up, me one down. Imbued as he surely was with the precepts of the men's movement, the search for release from such games, he nonetheless triggered them.

The exchange between us might seem innocuous, and perhaps I make too much of it, but I think a slow motion replay allows us to see the role played by the unconscious, the complexes activated and the reflexive behaviors that tie men to no-win positions. A complex is an emotionally charged cluster of energy in the psyche. We may or may not be aware of such psychic charges, but when activated they have the power to temporarily take over the conscious personality. Thus, the situation itself—two men meeting, sizing each other up— activated the complexes and, against our conscious intent, we played out historically-charged roles. On the collective level, men play out this competitive and shaming exchange daily, whether in academic or corporate turf wars or on the high seas and battlefields.

In sizing each other up, as men do when they meet, the shadow of the power complex inevitably surfaces. The shadow represents that part of our psyche with which we may be uncomfortable, or disdain, or that threatens ego intentions, but serves as a split-off part of the soul nonetheless. Working with the shadow represents the only way of integrating it, for what is not integrated will be projected onto others or leak out in dangerous behavior. While the encounter of two men on the streets of Santa Fe is hardly an epic confrontation, still it constellates the archetypal problem of power with all its attendant fears and defenses.

This leads us to the second male secret, that *men's lives are essentially governed by fear.*

Because men cannot undo what fragile strength they have assembled, they can scarcely admit to themselves or others how much fear influences them. But the healing of a man will require that he cease feeling shamed by his fear. I have always admired the freedom of women to acknowledge their fears, to share them, and thereby reap the support of others. For a man to so acknowledge the place of fear in his life is to risk feeling unmanly and to expect shaming by others. So his isolation deepens.

But this secret is out, fellows. Even your women are on to you, indeed they always have been. While researching this book, I came across an article in the March 1992 issue of, yes, *Ladies Home Journal:* "Men's Secret Fears: What He'll Never Tell You." So they have found us out. In essence the article correctly identifies men's two fundamental fears, the fear of not measuring up and the fear of physical or psychological trial. (Notice the latent expression of the twin worries I discovered in childhood, work and war).

The fear of not measuring up is the Saturnian shadow at its most obvious—competition, winners-losers, productivity as the measure of manhood. The fear of trial, the fifth phase of the initiatory rites, is expressed by men who doubt their ability to defend themselves and their family. How many films, from *Straw Dogs* to *Cape Fear,* have stirred this caveman in us, defender of the hearth? Indeed, many men confide that they are more afraid of illness, incapacity and impotence than of death. When I have said as much to an audience—on the logical face of it absurd, for what could be more frightening than death?—invariably men have nodded their heads. Yes, they are more afraid of the trial, of failing the ordeal, than of death itself. Impotence, powerlessness in any of its forms, is worse than annihilation. Work, war and worry.

Governed as he is by fear, unable to admit this to himself lest his hold on things slip, unable to share with his comrades lest he be shamed, a man compensates. The man who boasts of his big car, or big house, or big position with a big title, is surely compensating to some degree for how small he feels. Upscale lunches and power over others may serve an edifice complex, but they are pathetic substitutes for genuine empowerment. As that late great American philosopher Pearl Bailey expressed it, "Thems what thinks they is, ain't." Beneath displays of power is the complex; beneath the complex lies fear. No animal is more dangerous than one that is frightened. Perhaps Freud was right when he said that all things were sexual, or Adler in giving primacy to power, for when eros is injured it resorts to the gambit of power.

The power complex is the central force in the lives of men. It drives them and wounds them. Out of their rage they wound others, and out of their sorrow and shame they grow more and more distant from each other. The cost of this mutual wounding is enormous, repetitive and cyclic. Whatever is unconscious is internalized in debilitating ways or projected onto others and acted out destructively.

The cost of these first two secrets, that men's lives are as much governed by role expectations as women's, and that men are secretly ruled by fear, is rather easy to discern in the sufferings of individual men and the pathology of our society. American men die, on the average, eight years before women. They are four times more likely to be substance abusers and also four times more likely to take their own lives. They are eleven times more likely to spend time in jail.[17] And these statistics do not even begin to plumb the depth of male rage, male sadness, male isolation.

The men's movement is a welcome response to this suffering, which is both obvious and hidden. I would not demean the desire of men to create a safe space where they might gather together to share initiatory, life-deepening experiences. But I believe that ultimately change comes through the individual. Sharing has its place, but personal change is primary.

---

[17] See Aaron Kipnis, *Knights without Armor,* pp. 16ff.

Marxists have rightly critiqued the capitalist social structure most of us have grown up serving. Karl Marx, in my view, was a humanitarian who saw the evils of his day, and subsequently ours, and expressed not only his rage but his vision of the alternative—the classless society. Sadly, however, his vision is repudiated by the gulags, the pogroms and the thousand reminders that whosoever ignores the worth and weight of the individual will only create a new tyranny. In seeking to improve the material status of man, at the same time Marx devalued his spiritual status and thus created an edifice that would ultimately collapse. As we were told two thousand years ago, we do not live by bread alone.

Therefore, although valuing social action, I know that all institutions end by serving their own survival and not the cause for which they were founded. Similarly, although I value the necessity and the intentions of the men's movement, I also know that wherever two or three are gathered, there too is the shadow of power.

Accordingly, this book is written for individual men and for the women who stand in relationship to them. Join groups, share with other men, but it is in the smithy of the private soul that the modern man must be born. It is only through the capacity to discern what forces course within him that will determine a man's return, or not, to the organization, to the marriage, to the society at large, as part of the solution.

Jungian analyst James Hillman has recently criticized the long struggle for consciousness in an iconoclastic book, *We've Had a Hundred Years of Psychotherapy and the World Is Getting Worse.* His point is valid, but I believe that group action can be no more efficacious than the sum of individual consciousness brought to it. Men of good will have created bureaucratic monsters and institutions to torture others, spreading a terrible darkness. In his 1937 lectures at Yale Jung made an indelible point: the new man must bear the burden of the shadow consciously, for

> such a man knows that whatever is wrong in the world is in himself, and if he only learns to deal with his own shadow he has done something real for the world. He has succeeded in shouldering at least an

infinitesimal part of the gigantic, unsolved social problems of our day. These problems are mostly so difficult because they are poisoned by mutual projections. How can anyone see straight when he does not even see himself and the darkness he unconsciously carries with him into all his dealings?[18]

Thus, in the following pages, I invite individual men to reflect on those forces that contend within them. What we do not understand in ourselves is projected onto our surroundings, and so the sum of our society is the aggregate of what is unconscious in each of us. In sharing the dreams and dilemmas of individual men, I show how we are all personally affected by the same issues. The more fully we understand how we relate inwardly to the feminine, the more able are we to disentangle the skein of relationship with an actual woman. In understanding the necessary wounding of our sensibilities, we can suffer the world's monstrous pathologies without become monsters ourselves. In acknowledging our deep hunger for the tribal fathers, we can more nearly parent ourselves.

The roles and expectations, the shadow of Saturn, rest heavily on us all. We can continue to blame "them"—those who mysteriously invented and institutionalized all of this—but then nothing will change. We can no longer wait for something to change "out there," even with a men's movement afoot; we must change ourselves. All change starts within, but we men often have trouble internalizing our experience. So the task is difficult, but it is far preferable to living forever under Saturn's shadow.

---

[18] "Psychology and Religion," *Psychology and Religion,* CW 11, par. 140.

2

Dragon Dread:
The Inner and Outer Woman

The Greeks thought of Eros as a god, oldest and yet youngest of all the gods, at the beginning of all things and ever-renewing, ever-emergent. Eros driven underground becomes rage, and great violence ensues. Eros differentiated builds cathedrals and writes symphonies. We have too narrowly confined the work of this god within the bounds of sexuality. Surely he is present there, but we are moved by forces deeper than sex, longer than love, more mysterious than the beloved.

One of the best places to discern what Blake called "the lineaments of desire"[19] is in the poet. And perhaps no modern poet has taken us deeper than Rainer Maria Rilke. In his third "Duino Elegy" Rilke tracks the dark presences that course within men, contrasting songs to the beloved with "that hidden guilty river-god of the blood":

> How he devoted himself—. Loved.
> Loved what was inner in him, the wilderness of within,
> this jungle inside him, upon whose mute topple
> his heart stood, light-green. Loved. Left it, leapt
> beyond his own roots into enormous origin,
> where his little birth was already outlived. Loving,
> he had his descent into an older blood, into ravines,
> where what was dreadful lay, still fat with the fathers.
> And everything
> terrible knew him, blinked, appeared informed.
> Yes, what was horrible smiled. . . Seldom
> have you smiled so tenderly, mother. How should
> he not love it, since it smiled at him. He loved it
> *before* you, for even then, as you carried him, it was
> dissolved in the water that makes what is sprouting light.

---

[19] "A Question Answered," in *The Norton Anthology of Poetry,* p. 508.

> See, we don't love, as flowers do, out of a
> single year; where we love, immemorial sap
> mounts into our arms.[20]

The man sees the beloved, but can her visage alone so deeply stir? Behind her stands his caring mother who made harmless "the nightly frightening room." Yet even she serves to front for, mediate, the still deeper presence of "the torrents of ancestry." He senses "the wilderness of within," the "jungle inside." Down there, he knows, "where what was dreadful lay," something waits and smiles at him.

This primal encounter lives eternally in the soul of man, full of fear and tenderness. When we love, then, timeless juices rise through the veins. The beloved stirs and activates all this fear and desire, but is not its only carrier.

Rilke intuitively grasped what Jung has described, that life is enacted on three levels simultaneously: consciousness, the personal unconscious and the archetypal or collective unconscious. We vest much significance in our status as conscious beings, perhaps because consciousness is so hard won and because it constitutes the known. But the ego, the center of consciousness, is a thin wafer floating on an immense ocean. We all know this, intuitively and experientially, when we sleep or are stormed by uncontrollable complexes. But we seldom give sufficient weight to what courses within, thinking, perhaps, that what we do not know will not hurt us. This is worth repeating: what we do not know, controls us.

Beneath ego consciousness lies the personal unconscious, the sum of those things that have transpired since our birth. We may not remember them but they remember us. This is the realm of the personal complexes. Again, a complex is an emotionally charged experience, the power of which is a function of how large the original affective load, as in the case of a trauma, or how long its influence, as in the case of a relationship. Of all the experiences of life, normally the most important we ever have is of our mother. Certainly other experiences and relationships have an influence, but typically the experi-

---

[20] *Duino Elegies,* p. 47.

ence of the mother is psychologically determinative.

The personal mother is the source from which we emerge, having shared her blood, floated in her amniotic seas and resonated to her neurological network. Even after separation, we reflexively long for reconnection. In some way every act of life thereafter is eros seeking reconnection through other objects of desire, through sublimation, or even through projection onto the cosmos itself (hence the word religion, from Latin *religare,* "to bind back to or reconnect with"). Moreover the personal mother is the protector, nourisher and primary mediator between the fragile child and the larger world. (As Rilke noted, she mediates the darkness of the child's imaginal terrors.) She is the Primal Object standing over us, around us, and between us and the world. Is it any wonder that her significance looms so large?

One's mother incarnates and models the archetype of life. Though fathers contribute their chromosomal heritage, the mother is the place of origin, locus of parturition and omphalos of our world. Such "torrents of ancestry" are entrusted to the fragile vessel of a single person, a woman, who phenomenologically communicates the mystery of life itself and who, in the specific relationship between mother and child, embodies all sorts of messages about our relationship to the life force. The mother's biochemistry in utero, the treatment of the child by his mother, her affirmations or denials of his personhood, are primal messages to boys about their own being.

Just as human life emerged from the primordial seas, so we emerged from umbilical waters. How we are related to those origins and how we are to comprehend ourselves and our place in the cosmos are initially construed through the mother-child encounter. Not only do we share most of our early, formative days and years with her—the more so if fathers are distant or not there at all—but her role is replicated by teachers and other caretakers who in our culture are still primarily female. Hence the major influx of information men receive about themselves, and what life is about, comes from woman.

Whence derives the third great secret men carry, namely that *the power of the feminine is immense in the psychic economy of men.*

As one's personal mother is the bearer of the archetype of life, so we experience both a collective and a uniquely personal message. The mother complex, that is, the affectively charged idea of mother, is in us all. It is experienced as the longing for warmth, connection and nurturance. When one's initial experience of life met these needs, or largely so, one feels that one belongs in life, that here is a place where one will be nurtured and protected. Where the primal experience of the feminine was conditional or painful, one feels deracinated, disconnected. Such an ontological wound is felt in the body, burdens the soul and is frequently projected onto the world at large. One's entire Weltanschauung can derive from this largely unconscious, phenomenological "reading" of the world.

An example comes to mind of a woman I saw analytically. Cynthia was born in Germany during the early days of the war. Her biological mother, a gifted and sensitive artist, committed suicide when the child was two. Her biological father served in the Wehrmacht and was captured in North Africa. When he returned from captivity he did not feel up to parenting and turned his daughter over to his wife's sister; he died a year later in a cycling accident.

The stepmother had only reluctantly accepted her sister's child and never bonded with her. As a child, Cynthia stole chocolate and toys from stores even though her family was upper middle class. When she reached puberty Cynthia became severely anorexic and spent her adolescence in various clinics and hospitals. I met her when she was in her thirties. Her eating disorder persisted but was no longer life threatening. She was now bulimic, binging on chocolates and vomiting perhaps twice a week. She taught foreign languages in her home where she could control her environment and had had only a few brief, transient romantic relationships.

About ten months into therapy Cynthia dreamt that a witch had entered her apartment, stolen the doll she was holding and fled down the street. In the dream she felt extreme anxiety and pursued the kidnapper. When she caught up with the witch she tried to buy the doll back, but the witch refused. Cynthia pleaded and the witch replied that she would give the doll back if Cynthia would perform three tasks: 1) make love with a fat man, 2) deliver a public lecture at

Zürich University, and 3) go back to Heidelberg and have a sit-down dinner with her stepmother. The dream ended with Cynthia sadly acknowledging that, while she knew the performance of such tasks would free her captive doll, they lay beyond her powers. So, too, consciously, she felt intimidated by the tasks.

This dream is a compelling example of how we all experience the mother at the three levels simultaneously. The loss of her personal mother, the loss of a father who might also have nourished and protected her, and the experience of a most ambivalent surrogate, traumatized Cynthia at both the personal and archetypal levels. A witch is a common symbol of the negative mother and it is that experience of life which had, figuratively, stolen Cynthia's inner child, her doll. As a result her life became a defense *against* life, against risk and commitment. Her anorexia, and later bulimia, was a projection of that existential angst onto food.

The triple task imposed by the witch, who is experienced as such because she incarnates the destructive experience of Cynthia's life, would represent a symbolic liberation of those areas in her life where she is frozen. She was not to make love with a fat man literally, but seek to overcome her estrangement from her own body, the local repository of the archetype of nature. She was to deliver a lecture in order to overcome the agoraphobic defense against contacts with others. And she was to meet with the metonymical representative of her wounding, the stepmother, over, of all places, a meal, where the matter-*mater* wound might be healed.

Such a dream represents the effort of the psyche to heal itself. The child is born whole, but then is wounded by life events, each wound splitting off some natural truth and producing a concomitant strategy for survival. Such a split and attendant reflex is more popularly known as neurosis, the split between soul and society that each of us suffers. Again, while the dream is that of a woman, it illustrates well how the three levels of being are engaged and carry the trace of the initial encounters with the mother world.

At the conscious level Cynthia lived a life of self-protection. At the level of the personal unconscious, her eating disorder was a symbolic expression of her ambivalence toward food, the projection of the mother-wound onto matter (from Latin *mater,* mother). At the archetypal level Cynthia suffered estrangement from the body and from others because the first encounters with the Other had been contaminated. The strategically assembled reflexes that constituted her personality testify to the immense importance of the primal encounter with the Other, that the personal mother, for good or ill, mediates. Sadly, but inevitably, that relationship with the primal Other becomes paradigmatic for the child, who expands upon the datum fate has offered to define both self and world. When the encounter with the primal Other is more consistent and nurturant than Cynthia's was, the child will feel more grounded in his or her own reality and more trusting of the world around. As Freud once observed, the child who has the mother's devotion will feel invincible.[21]

But, alas, the devoted blessing of the mother can be a curse as well. Many women have sought to live out their unlived life through their sons. This is the source of so many "My son, the Doctor" jokes. In fairness to such women, their animus development—the inner masculine principle having to do with assertiveness, competency and empowerment—has often been blocked by cultural gender limitations. Hence they have tried to live out their empowerment vicariously through their sons. The psychic inflation in men that may result from having a devoted mother can even drive them to heights that by themselves they might never have attained.[22]

Jung suggested that perhaps the greatest burden for a child is the unlived life of the parent. Thus, the undeveloped animus of the mother often drives men, silently, unconsciously, to achieve. Even the hulking defensive end mouths "Hi, Ma!" when the portacam zooms in on him on the sideline. There is nothing intrinsically wrong with the man motivated by a strong mother presence. Yet we must ask how and to what extent he leads his own life if he is carrying the

---

[21] Ernest Jones, *The Life and Work of Sigmund Freud,* vol. 1, p. 8.

[22] See Mercedes Maloney and Anne Maloney, *The Hand That Rocks the Cradle,* a study that traces the role of the mother in the lives of many famous men.

projections of his parent. If men are to be liberated, they must, at the very least, make conscious the values they serve.

Behind such blind ambitions men are driven in darker ways by the power of the mother complex. Often the woman who has not lived our her own life, has not developed her own animus, tries to keep her son under her psychic dominance. Let me mention two worst-case but factual examples.

A former colleague on a college campus never married but, in his early fifties, took in his mother who had been born in the Old World. As she grew older she grew increasingly senile and wandered the campus on her own. On two occasions she locked her arms in the hallway doors and blocked the entrance. When asked why she had done this, she replied, "I am keeping the girls from my poor Sammy." She had managed her project very well and her son only married for the first time a few months after her death. So great was the enthrallment of the complex that a brilliant scholar and teacher could not free his psyche until he was freed by fate.

Another man, who was having considerable difficulties in his marriage, finally mustered the strength to ask his mother to butt out and allow him to work out his relationship with his wife without interference. He showed me her reply on a small piece of paper:

Dear Son,

You will never know how you have broken your mother's heart. Of the ten men who could have been your father, you will only have one mother. I do not have long for this earth, but I hope that I can have my son back before I die.

love, Your Mother

Some day there will be a Mother's Hall of Fame in which this letter belongs. It hits all the buttons: guilt for ruining her animus projection, denigration of the man's father and the implication that the son is responsible for her well-being. Rather than laugh at her overt heavy-handedness, or rage at the manipulation, the man felt crushed. "How," he asked, "am I to write back?" He was so completely under her psychic influence that he could not see through her; he could only passively suffer. Moreover, he had been so stripped of his own empowerment that he could not hold his half of the marital relationship. Her note, and their relationship, was not about love but about power. Again, as Jung noted, where power is, love is not.

Similarly, I have seen a considerable number of men in therapy whose need for mothering is so extensive that they are doomed to be dissatisfied with their wives. While it is clear that women do not want to be mothers to their husbands, it is also clear that many men seek in their wives the sort of unconditional acceptance and nourishment associated with positive mothers. Indeed, I have seen many men stuck in marriages that were dreadful for various reasons but they were unable to countenance the idea of leaving. Departure held all the terrors of the child leaving home for the unknown. Sexuality, in particular, is freighted with the infantile need for bodily contact and nurturance. As women grow weary of taking care of little boys, so little boys find it harder and harder to leave home and grow up, since neither father nor the fathers are available to show the way.

When men feel the push-pull of the mother complex they are apt to confuse that power with the outer woman in their life. Just as they often regress in intimate relationships, making a mother of their partner, unconsciously demanding she be "the good breast," so they fear and oppress women, as if by controlling them they might master the fear of their own undertow. The sorry history of men's treatment of women is stark testimony to this. *One oppresses what one fears.* Fear is responsible for the oppression of women and for gay bashing, the latter most notably by young men insecure in their own psychological reality. The resistance President Clinton encountered in proposing to end the ban on homosexuals in the American military was not because there were no homosexuals already serving bravely and honorably, nor because regulations regarding sexual harassment were not already in place, but because of the macho man's fear of his own feminine side.

Machoism is in direct proportion to man's fear, and the banding together of fearful men is the breeding ground of violence and the tacit admission of the power of the feminine in their lives. Vast bastions of macho mentality remain in contemporary society, perhaps none more regressive than the military. Possibly, in order to do the work of killing, a man has to override every principle of relatedness within him; he can ill afford to pay attention to doubt or to the eros principle. In his frightened heart he knows what the Greeks made clear long ago, that in the end Ares (Mars) was no match for Aphrodite (Venus). But he will fight her power because, sadly, he has not yet learned that to be a man is to feel comfortable with his feminine side as well. Because his fear is only partly conscious, it is projected onto women and gays, among others. In his unreasoning fear, the macho man remains a little boy just as much as the man who expects all women to mother him. Both of them have unwittingly succumbed to the power of the mother experience and denied that same large power within themselves.

Surely the greatest tragedy for men in regard to the feminine principle is that their fear alienates them from their own anima, the principle of relatedness, feeling and connection to the life force. This alienation from self obliges alienation from other men as well. Often their only connection with each other comes through superficial talk about outer events, such as sports and politics.

Recently I was in a neighborhood barbershop getting my hair cut. A man swaggered in and announced at the top of his voice, "The dumbest thing, my wife just said I should go see a therapist!" No one responded. He thought no one had heard him so he repeated the sentence, but still no one answered. In the past, perhaps, he would have evoked the anticipated Greek-chorus response that, yes, surely that was the dumbest thing anyone ever heard. Apart from slouching further into my chair, I concluded that the others were probably thinking what I was: "She's got a good idea there, buddy." In retrospect the scene, typical of thousands like it, seems rather amusing, but I believe that beneath the man's attempt to find reassurance in a male enclave crouched his deep-seated fear.[23]

---

[23] As I write these sentences on a Super Bowl Sunday, I read in the newspaper that today is the single most common day of wife-battering. If the allegation is even partly true, it is shameful and illustrative of the fear men dump on women on this most macho of days.

Jungian analyst Guy Corneau points out that men grow alienated from their own bodies as well, for they associate their corporeal reality with the early, primal contact with the mother.[24] As they were seldom held and hugged by their fathers, they correlate matter with mother, and disconnect from their bodies. For this reason men visit their physicians only one quarter as often as do women—perhaps one reason why men die earlier. Yes, it is true that men feel obliged to overrule their bodies frequently in physical or cerebral labor, but they do so at their peril. It is easy enough to blame outer conditions, but we collude in our self-alienation because of this deep ambivalence toward the mother-materia that clothes our bones and sinews.

The classical story of the archer Philoctetes is illustrative of the dilemma of modern men. His story comes to us from Greek mythology, in a play by Sophocles in 409 B.C.E. In return for his funereal service to the hero Heracles, Philoctetes is given the fabulous bow which shoots poisonous arrows that never miss their mark. En route to the plains of Troy Philoctetes is bitten by a serpent. The resulting wound will not heal. Finally his shipmates can no longer stand the odor of the suppurating bite and his cries of anguish, so they abandon him on an island for nearly ten years while the blood bath at Troy continues. After a prophecy that they could not take the fabled city without the help of the wounded archer, the Greeks send an emissary to woo him back to their ranks. Feeling betrayed, Philoctetes spurns their entreaties. He wishes to retreat into his cave, amid his pain and loneliness, and wait for death. The chorus, representing collective wisdom, urges him to reconsider and choose heroic engagement over selfish exile, but he persists in his refusal. Finally he experiences a vision of Heracles urging him to return to the fray. He does so, slays Paris, and is instrumental in the fall of the citadel.

Sophocles' play has often been interpreted as dramatizing the conflict between the individual and the demands of society. But we go deeper if we recognize that, while Philoctetes certainly had reason to feel betrayed by his comrades, his response was essentially narcis-

---

[24] *Absent Fathers, Lost Sons,* p. 23.

sistic. A narcissistic wound occurs when one's core sense of self is damaged and, as a result, one tends to view the world through that gestalt only. Such a person is "wound-identified." Philoctetes' war, for instance, is less with the Trojans or his Greek comrades than with his own progressive versus regressive impulses. Before he can come to terms with his society and its demands, he must come to terms with his own rage and the enormous desire to retreat into loneliness, pain and self-pity. His vision of Heracles is the projection of that which is heroic in himself. His healing will come only by engaging fully in life, not in retreating from it. The cave into which he would repair is in fact his own mother complex, the place of comforting darkness, warm and wet with pity and solicitude.

In myth, religious tradition and cultural patterns we see the movement of archetypal forces. We discern what is timeless in our human condition. We are stunned by the shock of recognition, humbled by our small part or ennobled by the summons to a great drama that courses within us even as it fashions, and fashioned, world history. Mythic motifs show us how the ancients intuitively discerned the dilemmas of humankind. It is no accident that the parents of modern depth psychology, Freud and Jung, turned frequently to myth to learn and describe the movement of those invisible energies that shape history through the acts of individuals.

The serpent motif, for example, reveals a rich ambivalence. The serpent was associated with the mysteries of nature, with the Great Mother, for its whole length was in contact with that primal source, the earth. As such, the serpent embodied the mysteries of the great cycle of life and death. On the one hand, as a denizen of the depths, it invited regression; on the other, it sheds its own skin, knows the secrets of healing and renewal. At the sanctuary of Asclepius at Epidaurus the pilgrim in search of healing took warm baths, symbolic of regression to the womb, and waited upon dreams or the bite of serpents from the lower world. Such visitations helped bring body and soul back into relationship with the Great Mother. Accordingly, the serpent's bite is analogous to the dual aspect of the mother, that archetypal force which gives both gives life and seeks to take it back.

A man's life teeters on that fine edge between regression and progression, between annihilation and individuation. He yearns for the cessation of the psychic stress which begins at birth, while the whole impetus of his genetic inheritance is toward the realization of his potential, both as an individual and as a part of his culture.

D. H. Lawrence captured the resulting tension well in a poem titled "Snake."[25] While visiting a well in Sicily, the speaker in the poem encounters a serpent sunning itself. He is fascinated by the encounter with the Other, but:

> The voice of my education said to me
> He must be killed . . . .
> And voices in me said, If you were a man
> You would take a stick and break him now, and finish him off.

He wrestles with his admiration of the natural being, and yet those voices implore: "If you were not afraid, you would kill him!" Fear and admiration vie in his soul. Then the serpent, slowly, deliberately, begins to slide back down into "the dark door of the secret earth." The poet is filled with a sense of horror at the idea of one who was "deliberately going into the blackness." At that moment he flings a log at the snake to break the tension. Immediately he regrets his impulsiveness: "How paltry, how vulgar, what a mean act!" His self-judgment is harsh:

> And so, I missed my chance with one of the lords
> Of life.
> And I have something to expiate:
> A pettiness.

Thus the ambivalence of men toward the underworld. They are both fascinated and frightened. Back there lie origins and healing, they sense, but also annihilation. So they fling the logs of fear and the chance for rapprochement passes.

When I was a child my grandfather, who once rode the western plains, persuaded me that his navel was where an Indian arrow had

---

[25] In *Norton Anthology of Poetry,* pp. 952-954.

once pierced him. While puzzled that I had a similar wound, I believed him wholeheartedly. Intuitively, he was right. It is the world's wound, the omphalos spun tight from the solar plexus, the trace and track of disconnection we all carry. Such a wound obliges one to undertake this exile from the source which is our lives. It obliges separation, irrevocable and omnipresent, as well as isolation and prolonged suffering. When men feel the wound that cannot heal, they either bury themselves in a woman's arms and ask her for healing, which she cannot provide, or they hide themselves in macho pride and enforced loneliness. In the story of Philoctetes, the chorus explains to him the universality of this wound and that he still must live his life, but he wraps himself in pain and self-pity. This regressive move is only overcome by the vision of Heracles urging his return to the battle. This is the encounter with the hero archetype.

The hero archetype is present in us all. It is the inherent capacity to mobilize the energies which serve life, to overthrown the demons of despair and depression. Incarnating this archetype has little to do with outer feats; rather it manifests when one summons the energy to confront fear, pain and the regressive attraction of the womb. We may admire heroic accomplishments, but we should never worship a hero. The psyche continually prods us to make something of ourselves. This is an heroic task that awaits our response.

At the beginnings of all peoples there is a myth of the primal act, or genesis, from which all else stems. In the life of the individual, this event is the severing of the maternal connection. Similarly, each people has its mythos of a fall, loss of the paradisical connection preceding consciousness. Perhaps this racial memory is only the neurological, phylogenetic trace of the trauma of birth separation. But out of this separation comes the experience of duality.

Thus begins the spiral of consciousness, an ever-developing process that is founded on the experience of subject and object, and occasions the pain of ever-further distance from the primal connection. The growth of conscious culture, in the life of the tribe or of the individual, brings the fruits of civilization but, as well, greater and greater estrangement from the Great Mother.

Every day we stand poised on the razor's edge of consciously suffering the world's wound. How great the temptation to hide in a cave or to sink into some comforting arms. Each morning the grinning gremlins of fear and lethargy return. It does not matter how boldly we sallied forth yesterday; they are back today and, not satisfied to nibble our toes, will gobble our souls if we let them. Thus, we have evolved elaborate ways to avoid the pain of further consciousness Many remain infantile in their thoughts, emotions and actions. Some turn to the soporifics of drugs and alcohol. Still others turn to ideologies, simple-minded -isms, religions or socio-political views that offer black and white answers to complex questions, thereby relieving one of the struggle with the tension of opposites.

At the same time, the life force surges within each culture and each individual. This powerful eros seeks its connection ahead, not behind. It requires the activation of the hero archetype within a society and within individuals. It was the task of the great religions and rites of passage to guide men through the nexus of lethargy and progression, but today, most men are left to find their own path. Society still depends on them to undertake this challenge, for no society can prosper if its men are immature.

Sometimes, knowing he cannot return to the womb, a man will project that yearning onto the cosmos. The culture of Romanticism was much given to this *Sehnsucht für Ewigkeit,* or "yearning for eternity." One senses it in, for instance, the myth of Empedocles, who flung himself into the crater of Etna, and the paintings of Kaspar David Friedrich, notably *The Wanderer Above the Mists.* Thanatos, the longing for extinction, is poised always against eros, the life force. Historically, mystics have sought to describe the indescribable, consistently reporting two characteristics: the mystical experience is essentially ineffable and involves a merging with the All.

But, far more often, men seek their reconnection to the cosmic, primal source through a relationship. As mentioned earlier, the feminine is experienced by a man on three levels. He encounters it in the presence of an outer woman and in gay relationships through the feminine side of the other man. He meets it in his relationship to his own anima. And he encounters it in his relationship to the archetypal world, his relationship to nature, to his instinctual center and to the life force in general.

In any relationship a man is largely at the mercy of what he does not know about himself. And the extent to which he is in the dark is the degree to which his own inner woman is projected onto another person. Since projection is by definition a dynamic whereby unconscious contents are experienced as outer, a man is always falling in love with, or fearing, his own unconscious material.

We recall that normally the personal mother is the primary mediator of our experience of the feminine. Rilke plays on this truth in his third "Duino Elegy," quoted at the beginning of this chapter. Another poet, Stephen Dunn, recalls how his mother, at his request, revealed her breast to him. Gently, modestly and lovingly she assuaged his curiosity and his fears, and that experience, writes Dunn, "I think permits me / to love women easily."[26]

For other men, the early mediation by the mother was less gentle, less reassuring. The authors who coined the term "serial killers" note that all of the dozens of mass murderers they studied (only one of whom was female) had disturbed childhoods. Always their crimes were sexually motivated, whether a sexual act was attempted or not. Their fear and rage were mostly directed against women, with whom they felt incapable of forming bonds of warmth. Richard Speck is a typical example. When he could not sustain an erection while raping the Chicago nurses, he killed them.[27]

Recently an analysand reported that a co-worker had tried to run her over with a car. He also had physically barred her from entering a room at their place of employment he considered his territory. Once they had dated and cuddled. When she sought to deepen the relationship, his behavior turned increasingly rude and then violent. This is not uncommon. Many men are full of rage against women, and often

---

[26] "The Routine Things Around the House," in *Not Dancing*, p. 40.
[27] Robert Ressler and Tom Schactman, *Whoever Fights Monsters*, pp. 79-81.

they act it out. Their rage is in some cases the product of child abuse and quite easy to identify etiologically in terms of cause and effect. But many times the rage is because of too much mother and not enough father as a balance. Their rage is of course the accumulation of anger, the epiphenomenal emotion that occurs when the psychic territory of the child is violated. When this fragile boundary is repeatedly breached, either by abuse or by too much interference in the child's development, the nascent ego suffers permanent damage and may become sociopathic.

The sociopath cannot form a caring relationship with others. A man's experience of the primal relationship may have been so painful that he expects all relationships can only be painful. Thus his life is a dreary cycle of fearing domination by others and seeking to exploit them instead. Many a woman has set out to change such a man and found herself the victim of abuse. As his personality is a protection from his pain, he cannot bear to turn within and suffer that pain, thereby lifting it off the Other. Sadly, that historic pain becomes the constant buffer between himself and others. No matter what his external accomplishments, he is a terribly frightened man. He is so frightened that he cannot bear to look at his pain and can only see the Other as the source or continuance of it.

It is not my intention here to blame mothers (nor will fathers be blamed later), but it is necessary to acknowledge that the affectively charged imago of the feminine is considerably influenced by the experience of the personal mother and by the early experience of the nurturant environment. The anima is an archetypal energy in all men. It is essentially a mode of experiencing and relating, rather than a particular kind of knowledge. Influenced by relationships with outer women and by the culture (which Madonna is in vogue, for instance, the Virgin of Chartres or the virgin of erotica), a man's incarnation of the inner feminine is a function of how he stands in relation to the life force that courses within him, and how much he is at the mercy of its shifting moods.

I shall never forget the man who, dragged into therapy by his wife, walked in, sat down, noticed a box of tissues and said, with a smirk, "I see you had a woman here last hour." Factually, he was correct, but I did not want to concede his point. "Men can weep too," I said. "But they don't have too," he replied, "they can work it out." I countered: "Many men carry a mountain of rage and a lake of tears, and if they don't let it out it will kill them." He smirked again, as if to say, "You're a fool, like them." When I asked him what he was afraid of, he said only that he felt he had to keep his wife in line because she was the one who had problems. As one might predict, his "therapy" did not continue.

Generally speaking, a boy can suffer "too muchness" and "too littleness." As illustrations of the latter, I think of two men.

Joseph's life revolved around a single, and signal, event. When he was eight his mother announced she was leaving. He stood in the door of their home and watched her get in a car with a strange man and drive away forever. He never saw her again. His father refused to discuss her and continued his alcoholic retreats from his pain. Joseph grew up feeling abandoned. Never facile in school, he did learn to support himself and when he came to me he was the manager of a small manufacturing business. He came to therapy on his own volition; in fact, I was the third therapist he had visited. He had taken his wife to a therapist two years earlier "to get her straightened out." When that seemed to fail, they jointly visited a second therapist whom he insisted hypnotize his wife "to get at the truth." Although Joseph believed that his wife loved him and their two children, he was obsessed with the idea that she was having casual affairs, quick and indiscriminate, whenever the opportunity arose.

While the therapist is partly at the mercy of what the client chooses to communicate (and certainly affairs are not unknown within marriage), Joseph's examples of his wife's adultery cast considerable doubt on their probability. For example, on one of their wedding anniversaries they rented a room in a hotel in one of the Atlantic City casinos. While he was taking a shower room service arrived. Joseph was convinced that his wife knew the waiter and had had a quick liaison during those few minutes. His proof was that she "looked suspicious." Similar examples were forthcoming, each possible but requiring a stretch of the imagination. At his request, I interviewed his wife in private. She confirmed her commitment to the marriage and wondered why he was always so suspicious

The power of the invisible, of the ineluctable energy of the unconscious, is clearly seen in Joseph's dilemma. He had seen Her, his mother's, disappearing back, and from that single traumatic event had concluded that he could not count on Her.

The psyche often functions analogously, saying, "I have been here before." Rationally, the current situation may have nothing to do with what happened in the past, but the linkage is there emotionally. Joseph's wife became that feminine, intimate Other who held his well-being in her hands. As she was capable of loving him, so in his mind she was capable of infidelity, of taking off with another man— just as his mother had. His mother complex embroidered the facts, reaching the anticipated, dreaded conclusion that this woman, too, would leave him.

Joseph's psychic life was organized around that charged imago of "She who left—and will again." However grossly unfair this was to his wife, he could not help but replay the fantasy, in accord with what is known psychoanalytically as "reaction formation." Better the devil you have known than the ambiguity and tension of the unknown. Memory replayed the same sad, terrifying scenario—abandonment—in spite of the overt presence of his wife. The complex asserted its autonomy over the rational mind and constructed its own reality. So great was Joseph's wound, and the defenses around it, that he quit therapy when he could not receive confirmation of his wife's betrayal.

Another man, Charles, suffered the loss of his father when he was young. His mother went into a depression lasting years, leaving Charles feeling doubly abandoned. His later relations with adult women followed the pattern of the *puer aeternus,* the man who has not grown out of his mother need.[28] He would idealize women, put

---

[28] See, for instance, Marie-Louise von Franz, *Puer Aeternus: A Psychological Study of the Adult Struggle with the Paradise of Childhood,* and Daryl Sharp, *The Secret Raven: Conflict and Transformation.*

them on a pedestal, and then, once they were committed to the relationship, he would pull away and protect himself. Women who experienced this understandably withdrew themselves in puzzlement and sometimes anger. Charles seemed genuinely dumbfounded by their reaction, for he felt they should have understood and that he had done nothing to push them away.

In fact, his mother was the one he wished had understood his childhood need for nourishment and consistency, even in the face of her own grief, and how he as a child was paying twice. Again, the wound was so deep to the child that the adult, as with Joseph, continued to see the fault "out there," in women in general. Accordingly, rather than recognize the psychodynamic he brought to relationships, his goal in therapy was simply to refine his choice of women. He found it very difficult to acknowledge that the pattern of false idealization, ambivalence, rejection and abandonment was set up inside himself and projected onto every woman he met.

Naturally, without a capacity for introspection, one is doomed to live in a world created by projection and, no surprise, find one's fantasy, and worst fears, reflected back. Ever and always, what we have not owned within will be projected without.

One last example may suffice. Stephen grew up with immigrant parents who worked very hard in their store to "make it" in America. They faced not only the rigors of a new culture, but the difficulties of making any business survive during the thirties and forties. Stephen worked long hours beside his parents but never felt nurtured by them. They were always up against the odds, all of them, and he was, as children have often been historically, part of the family survival network without his own needs being addressed.

In his adult life Stephen married and remarried and had affairs, but never felt satisfied. His wound was similarly that of abandonment, and every woman he became close to was expected to make up the tragic deficit of his childhood. Of one mistress, he said that what he most enjoyed was cuddling with her, lying on her abdomen. When she wanted sex he was afraid of her demands. The scene he depicts is actually that of Madonna and child, safe and warm, far from the tough streets and hard times of the past.

Stephen was forever angry with the women in his life; he controlled them through money and threats, and felt they were using him. Again, the very deep pattern was that She was not there for him. His narcissistic void was of such magnitude that no woman could fill it, even the most co-dependent mothering Other he could find. Thus Stephen's life was characterized by sadness, for he was the chronically undernourished child desperately seeking a partner who would offer the cosmic nurturance of the Great Mother. Meanwhile he became a bully, full of rage and demanding compliance. Again, the same sad cycle plays itself out. Whether the man tries to make his partner the nurturant Other, that is, the mother, or fears the magnitude of his own need and defends himself against her, in all ways he testifies to the power of the mother complex.

In describing the pervasive influence of the anima, Jung alluded to the novel *She* by H. Rider Haggard, wherein the hero encounters "She who must be obeyed." Television viewers can see a comic take on this in the PBS series "Rumpole of the Bailey," where the crusty old actor Leo McKern, after besting the Queen's finest before the bar, shudders when he hears the stentorian "Rumpole!" of his wife and dejectedly mutters, "She who must be obeyed."

Again, recall that the anima is an archetype, that is, a psychic pattern which mediates man's relationship to instinct and to the life force. The encounter with the personal mother inevitably colors and conditions a man's relationship to his own anima, but too often the child's experience dominates the man's psychology. Loren Pederson summarizes the task:

> One of a man's greatest developmental tasks is to achieve a healthy separation from the bond with his personal mother. He must also develop an awareness of the importance of the image of the archetypal mother . . . . Unlike the daughter, the son lacks a primary identification with his mother, especially as he begins to psychologically emerge from her. In adult life, remnants of the original attachment/ separation problem are conveyed by a man's internal anima image.[29]

---

[29] *Dark Hearts: The Unconscious Forces That Shape Men's Lives*, p. 74.

The man who fantasizes that his wife is cavorting with another, the man who acts out his ambivalence toward his intimate partner, the man who rages at his inadequately nourishing wife, the man who telephones his wife from every truck stop or airport, controls the bankbook and claims his wife incompetent with finances, the man who has an incessant roving eye, who puts women down and attacks gays, the man who tries to please his partner at his own expense—all have not yet left home. They are attached still to the mother-son experience, out of touch with their own soul.

When we remember that patriarchy is a cultural contrivance, an invention to compensate for powerlessness, we realize that men, contrary to widespread opinion, are more often the dependent sex. The Marlboro Man, the rugged individualist, is most ambushed by his inner feminine, for he is most in denial. Whenever a man is obliged to be a good boy, or conversely when he feels he must be a bad boy, or a wild man, he is still compensating for the power of the mother complex.

I do not say it is a man's fault that he is so vulnerable, so dependent; that is merely human. What *is* his responsibility is to recognize how deeply any child needs positive mothering and how much the pattern of that need sets his psychic life in motion and continues to operate beneath the surface. He may pretend to adult empowerment, hold the reins of government or the purse, but the lines of stress reach deep down into his relationship with his mother. Men must grasp and accept this fact, and then take responsibility for it, or they will continue to play out infantile patterns forever.

The following diagram, adapted from Jung's explanation of what is going on psychologically in therapy, in terms of transference and countertransference, shows the variety of exchanges that take place in any heterosexual relationship.[30]

---

[30] For a fuller discussion of these dynamics, see my *Middle Passage,* pp. 46-47, and Daryl Sharp, *The Survival Papers: Anatomy of a Midlife Crisis,* pp. 70ff. (For Jung's original description and diagrams of the "cross-cousin marriage," see "The Psychology of the Transference," *The Practice of Psychotherapy,* CW 16, pars. 422ff.)

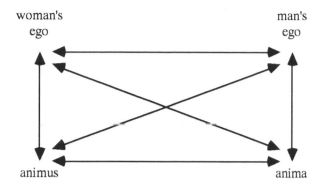

Although the relationship may play itself out on the conscious level, each person is informed by the contents of his or her unconscious, suggested by the vertical axes. The experience of falling in love happens when the Other lines up, if only for the time being, with one's inner image of the beloved. The Other seldom if ever can measure up to this expectation, so one regularly falls out of love. The man's relationship to the beloved can never be better than his relationship to his own anima, because what is unconscious in him will be contaminating his relationship with the Other, just as the Other is projecting onto him in turn.

While the anima has archetypal roots, recall that the mediation of that experience is essentially by way of the personal mother, then by other females in the boy's life and by the images available in his surrounding culture. Thus Stephen rages at his wife for not mothering him, though consciously he does not think he is so dependent. And George styles himself as the perfect husband because of his solicitousness toward his wife, yet inside he still is seeking to serve Her, win Her favor, be Her good child.

To the extent that men are unaware that the anima is within, they search for Her in other women, flee Her, oppress Her, ask Her to be Beatrice in their underworld, anesthetize Her pain through work or drugs. They overlook the presence of Her in their dreams, in their soul's flight, in the company of other men, in camaraderie with women, in art and music and sport, and in their fantasies and transient madness. The man who denies that the mother-child relationship is fundamental, that it influences everything he feels about himself, about life and about others, lives in profound ignorance. And, of course, that of which he is ignorant will be projected onto others. Even his deepest sexuality is fueled by this projection. When he is with Her, connected again, however transiently, he is home.

Most men consider the conditions of their working life a daily battering. No perks, no car, no key to the executive washroom, and even no raise will assuage the daily loss of soul. A man understands, deep down, that he is selling his soul, and no paycheck is large enough to compensate. Thus, upon the fragile, tactile connection with a woman, or the anima of another man, he places his soul's burden. "Take care of it, reassure it, bring it home, if only for awhile." Then, *post coitum triste,* he is disconnected again, adrift, at the mercy of the world and its battering.

Under the eyelids each morning, as he rose from the depths of sleep to face another day, one man reported feeling that he was back in high school playing football. The line was poised, and in that moment, before the snap of the ball, before the shock and collision of economic life, he fantasized always of sex. Another man, whose mother had been absent-spirited and rejecting, charged his anima with addictive longing for Her. He insisted his wife make love every day until, finally, she rebelled. He felt all the hurt and rejection again, and a vague sense of impending death. "Each time we make love," he said, "I feel I buy a day back from death. Each day we don't, I feel death has crept a little closer."

For both these men, sex served as reassurance and reconnection, rather than as an experience of communication and intimacy. It was, symbolically, their religion. For the former man the battering continued; the constant fantasy of sex with anyone along the way served as a pallid palliative to the soul's scars. For the latter, his ability to see that he was actually making his wife into a surrogate mother helped him pull back the projection. His sexuality grew less compulsive, more relaxed, less performance oriented, and the tenderness of their relationship returned. His realized that his unconscious angst had such urgency that he had driven his wife away. When he could own his inner child's distress and his compulsive urge to merge, the relationship regained its normal proportions.

Unless a man can acknowledge his dependency, which is to say the dependency of the child within, he will either flounder in an unhealthy relationship with a mother-surrogate or be angry that his partner does not measure up to his demands. Most men would be ashamed to admit that they seek their mother through their partner, but if they cannot separate their childhood relationship with the mother from their current relationship, they will be replaying an old, regressive script.

Jung has written quite eloquently of this large, indeed mythic, drama that courses through a man's soul. To become a conscious, adult being, he must struggle mightily with his mother complex, recognizing the battle as an internal one. Otherwise he will certainly project it outward onto women, either succumbing to their direction or seeking to dominate them—both testimonies to the power of the mother complex. In either case he realizes his deepest fear and his deepest longing—annihilation in the mother.

The dread and yearning for annihilation, writes Jung, is a powerful, personified "spirit of regression":

[It] threatens us with bondage to the mother and with dissolution and extinction in the unconscious. For the hero, fear is a challenge and a task, because only boldness can deliver from fear. And if the risk is not taken, the meaning of life is somehow violated, and the whole future is condemned to a hopeless staleness, to a drab grey lit only by will-o'-the-wisps.[31]

One cannot overemphasize the power of this dreadful longing for the womb; sustaining the consciousness to counter it is immensely painful. Adulthood, existential responsibility for one's survival and growth, is a Promethean prize wrested from the depths. Men may separate themselves from mother, from women, from their own anima, and think they are safe. Think again. Jung continues:

---

[31] *Symbols of Transformation,* CW 5, par. 551.

Always he imagines his worst enemy in front of him, yet he carries the enemy within himself—a deadly longing for the abyss, a longing to drown in his own source, to be sucked down to the realm of the Mothers. . . . [i.e., the archetypal depths]. If he is to live, he must fight and sacrifice his longing for the past in order to rise to his own heights. . . . Life demands that the young person should sacrifice his childhood and his childish dependence on the physical parents, lest he remain caught body and soul in the bonds of unconscious incest.[32]

Thus we see why our ancestors had such powerful rites of passage. They knew all too well the regressive power of the psyche, the longing for the safety and satiety of the Mother. The unconscious incest of Oedipus, the longing for peace of Philoctetes, the fascination of Faust for the realm of the Mothers—all such seductions men would blame on women, but their true origin lies in men's fear of life's pain and the lure of annihilation.

There is a way out of the labyrinth. Some men do escape the unconscious bonds to the Mother. They are liberated, not from Her, but from their submission to their own longing for rest and sanctuary. But only their daily courage and vigilance, their work on themselves, keeps them from slipping back.

Two examples of men involved in such work may help. One man, Lawrence, was raised by a narcissistically needy mother. His father served her, his sister served her, and Lawrence served her. When he left home he married a woman with a congenital illness whom he also served, little suspecting that in choosing this person he was maintaining his bondage to his mother. At midlife he developed a first-class depression. He left his wife, and, riddled with guilt, entered therapy. After nearly a year of writhing in the coils of remorse and indecisiveness over having relinquished his rescuing role, he had the following dream.

A woman is standing on a balcony looking at me. There is a yellow sports car there.
I jump in the car and drive away. Then I come to a lake and board a boat. I see a Greek temple under the water. There are trout there to

---

[32] Ibid., par. 553.

eat as well. Then I arrive at the other shore. There is a snake there with a bird in its mouth. I grab a knife and quickly cut off the head of the snake and save the bird. I have been bitten. Then the severed snake becomes a fish and I can eat it.

In his associations to the dream images Lawrence thought that the woman standing on the balcony was his mother, whose presence had brooded over him all his life. The yellow sports car embodied the sudden decision to leave her domination, to feel the full force and drive of self-determination. When he crosses the water, a ubiquitous symbol for the unconscious, he senses the great riches to be found there: ancient wisdom embodied in the temple, and food for the soul in the fish. Yet, on the other side, having left the personal mother, the archetypal mother awaits. The bird, suggestive of spirit and transcendent purpose, is still in peril from our old friend the serpent. Again the will, the masculine decisiveness, the phallic empowerment symbolized by the knife, permits him to divide his spirit's flight from the regressive serpent-complex.[33] The energy that might well have stayed lodged in the mother is then available for the journey of life. The regressive serpent becomes a potentially nourishing fish.

Another man, in his late fifties, carried an oppressive introjected imago of his mother as intervening and critical. For decades he had projected her enervating presence onto his employer, his intimates and the world in general. As a child his only defense was to avoid her, through fantasy and education. When he was seventeen he flew away from her courtesy of the United States Air Force. He avoided confrontation with others and lived an essentially isolated life-style. After some time in therapy he dreamt:

I take a little girl down to the dock to get on the Queen Elizabeth 2 for a voyage. But I can't find the ship this time. Then the scene changes. I am led into this wonderful house by a beautiful, helpful woman. This is the house of my dreams. White adobe with a spacious living room with a wonderful glass vista. On a glass coffee table there is a beautiful crystal vase with greens.

[33] For a book-length discussion of this theme see Robert L. Gardner, *The Rainbow Serpent: Bridge to Consciousness.*

This man had had many dreams of ocean voyages or air departures, all representative of his desire to flee, to avoid his mother's presence. Here he takes an immature anima figure to the mother ship (the complex). But he can't find it; there's no possibility of flight. Then a helpful, adult anima guides him to a beautiful house, reminiscent of Beatrice guiding Dante out of the underworld. He associated the Frank Lloyd Wright-inspired adobe house with the place of his potential being, his soul's Taliesin. He saw the beautiful crystal vase as a Holy Grail, a container of soul-enhancing psychic contents. The vase held rich greens, pointing to the life-giving side of the Great Mother.

It is tempting to make too much of such a dream, but it did seem to betoken a psychic shift. Since childhood, this man had felt dominated by others. The figure whose protection he had lacked as a child had instead intruded into his fragile psychic life, grievously wounding his eros, resulting in a destructive, devouring mother complex. His gradual understanding of the power of the mother, reflected in many life experiences, allowed him to withdraw the projection of Her onto other people and situations. In so doing, he gained a growing sense of his power to make choices and to live out the energies with which nature had endowed him.

No man can be himself until he has confronted the mother experience he internalized and carries into all subsequent encounters. Only through the courage to confront this potential abyss can he become independent and free of anger. If he still blames mother or women, he has not yet grown up; he still seeks the protection, or avoids the domination, of mother.

While my desire herein is not to blame but to describe in order to understand, the parents necessarily play a very large role in the burden the child will carry. Jung lays it out directly:

> What usually has the strongest psychic effect on the child is the life which the parents (and ancestors too, for we are dealing here with the age-old psychological phenomenon of original sin) have not lived. This statement would be rather too perfunctory and superficial if we did not add by way of qualification: that part of their lives which

might have been lived had not certain somewhat threadbare excuses prevented the parents from doing so. To put it bluntly, it is that part of life which they have always shirked ... [that] sows the most virulent germs.[34]

Our ancestors intuited this fact: what is not suffered, rendered conscious and integrated, is rolled over into the next generation. As Jung notes after the above remarks, "The curse of the House of Atreus is no empty phrase."[35] Moreover, he adds, "Nature has no use for the plea that one 'did not know.' "[36]

Thus, especially, the vagaries of the mother's personality, her level of consciousness, the character of her own wounding and attendant strategies, form the psychic inheritance of the child. She is that from which he draws so many messages about himself and about life and with whom he must come to terms. Even when her son is married and living with another woman she may play a determining role (to which the many mother-in-law jokes attest).

A crucial datum of human experience derives from the original birth separation.[37] Where had been connected to the heartbeat of the cosmos, all needs met, now the child is thrust alone into a world of gravity and a growing consciousness of radical relocation. The fragile human who becomes a mother bears a heavy archetypal weight. The child's experience of the personal mother creates the internalized experience of the feminine, that is, the mother complex. The phenomenological experience of the personal mother also conditions and colors the experience of life itself, of the encounter with all the natural forces, that is, the archetypal mother.

The absolute dependence of the child on its mother, or mother surrogate, is obvious. The vulnerability of the child occasions a primal separation anxiety that is unavoidable and ripples throughout the life

---

[34] "Introduction to Wickes's 'Analyse der Kinderseele,' " *The Development of Personality,* CW 17, par. 87.

[35] Ibid., par. 88.

[36] Ibid., par. 91.

[37] The phylogenetic memory of this separation may account for the fact that all peoples have their tribal account of a "fall," the collective memory of a lost paradisical state.

of the individual. Freud was right in asserting the primacy of eros, the urge to merge or reconnect, for the initial experience of life is of disconnection. All his life, then, a man seeks reconnection. Since he cannot go backward to Her, he must seek Her, or her symbolic substitute, out there in relationship with individuals or institutions, in ideologies or in the sky-parent, God.

In addition to the trauma of birth, the specific relationship of mother and child plays an immense role in a man's personal psychology. He is most likely to suffer one or both of two kinds of wounds. He will experience too much of her or not enough. In the former case the mother's needs, her unaddressed psychology, her wounds, her unlived life, will inevitably be imposed on the child. Her "too-much-ness" will flood his fragile boundaries and create in him a sense of powerlessness. This overwhelment will be carried into adult life, projected onto women and events in general, and his powerlessness will haunt him.

Similarly, a man may experience the inability of his mother to meet his needs and suffer a sense of abandonment. Inevitably, this diminishes one's inner sense of worth ("If I were better I would receive what I need and deserve"), resulting in a general insecurity as well as an addictive, angst-fueled search for Her. A man's sense of self is greatly affected by these wounds—overwhelment or abandonment or both.

As the child experiences the conditionality of his world, mediated by the mother encounter, so he suffers separation anxiety. This generalized anxiety, existential in scope and local in experience, modulates into a number of unspecific fears about himself, about others and about the feminine. These sundry fears are carried in the bones and repeatedly projected onto others. The Indo-Germanic root *angh* ("to constrict") gives rise to the English words angst, anxiety, angina and anger. Perceived threats to the well-being of the organism involuntarily and repeatedly occasion this range of emotions. The child instinctually, intuitively, knows what is needed and feels both anger at betrayal and sorrow at the loss of the necessary nurturant Other.

In an essay titled "Mourning and Melancholy," Freud noted that the overt loss of the Other, in death for example, produces grief. When the Other is not there for us emotionally, the loss is suffered but the object is still present. This cognitive dissonance produces sadness, or melancholy, driven inward but suffered throughout one's life. This silent suffering, this pathos, has produced some of the most exquisite expressions of longing in music, in art and in lyric poetry. The mood of the spiritual, "Sometimes I Feel Like a Motherless Child," is intuitively felt by everyone. Such a "longing for eternity" gave rise to the minnesingers in the Middle Ages, the later Romantic Movement and the great preponderance of mournful cowboy songs. Out there, somewhere, She waits.

For most men the dual wounding creates anger as well as grief. This anger is essentially unconscious, undifferentiated. There are four possible ways in which it might be processed. Feeling powerless, one may become depressed. Depression has been variously defined as "anger turned inward" and "learned helplessness." Or one may internalize that anger in the body, which may then combine with other physical circumstances to lead to illnesses such as gastric disorders, migraines, heart disease or cancer. Often the anger will leak out from the repression. What the boy could not express with the mother will surface in the man as general irritability. This is called "referred" or "displaced" anger and waits only for the slightest provocation to erupt in an objectively unwarranted rush of emotion (the prime indication of an activated complex).

Alternatively, a man may act out his anger in self-destructive behavior or violence toward others. Rape is widely known to be a crime not of lust but of violence, of referred anger. Violence toward women, in particular, is a function of the intensity of injury to a man's mother complex. Since the character and depth of the complex is essentially unconscious, a man can only attack what comes to him in some outer guise.

Even as an adult, every meeting with the outer feminine will be charged with this deep inner drama. Naturally, a man will transfer his fear of wounding and loss to his outer environment, even as his psyche carries those experiences within, as complexes. Intuiting the awesome power of such internalized history, and experiencing its potential reenactment in the present, the old fear resurfaces. He is driven by his childhood experience of the power of the feminine. In self-defense he will try to dominate or placate the outer Other. Hence the history of relationship between the sexes is a sad litany of men seeking to dominate and control because of their fear of the feminine within themselves. Whenever and wherever we see men seeking to control women, we are seeing fear's ugly work.

As a therapist I have witnessed this fear operating in the one-sided power balance of many marriages. Seeing the man adamantly controlling family finances and decision making, I have appealed to reason, common sense and fair play, only to run up against some irrational ground of resistance. In his heart of hearts he might truly like to give in, to relinquish his power, but he is dominated by fear of the consequences. Fear's ugly work created the patriarchy and, as Blake noted, "blights with plague the marriage hearse."[38]

On the other hand, and just as often, a man controlled by fear may seek ways to please and placate. He tries to keep Her happy, often sacrificing his own well-being in the process. Or he indulges the double urge to get his own way and still avoid confrontation through passive-aggressive behaviors that seek control and revenge.

One man became a very successful dentist, largely to please his mother and to replace his weak father in her affections. But he became a profligate spendthrift and finally drove himself into bankruptcy. Even he was dumbfounded by the apparent contradiction between earning nearly a quarter of a million dollars a year and being penniless. It came as a great revelation one day when he blurted out, "I became a dentist for her, but I screwed it all up for me." Feeling the oppressive power of his mother's ambitions, he sought his revenge in a passive-aggressive revolt. He succeeded only in his own ruination.

For another man, when his father died the full brunt of caring for his mother fell on him. When she made unreasonable, unceasing de-

---

[38] "London," in *Norton Anthology of Poetry*.

mands on him, demands that repeatedly invaded his marriage, insulted his wife and violated his privacy, the man turned his anger on his wife, charging her with insensitivity to his mother in her hour of greatest need—and stifled his own rage. He came to therapy because his wife and children complained about his sudden outbursts of anger. These discharges of emotion were seemingly in excess of the situations and were, of course, tapping into the reservoir of fear and rage he had carried his whole life. To direct his anger toward his mother, whose narcissistic needs respected no boundaries, seemed to him futile. The collision of fear and rage he felt toward his mother led him to rationalize her behavior and express anger toward his wife, whom he felt coerced him to deal with the issue. His wife had rightly felt a rival throughout their marriage, and it is fair to say that in not dealing with the power of his mother complex the man had redirected the blame for his anguish onto his wife. Psychologically, he had never left home.

Until a man becomes conscious of the effects of his mother complex, he will suffer troubled relationships. His anguish and anger will be internalized at his own expense, or projected at the expense of others. Until he becomes conscious of the lattice-work of history he carries within, he has not grown up. All the neediness of the inner child remains active in the present, as well as his fear of the mother's power to overwhelm or abandon him. This is why so many men seek to control their partner, for they feel the Other, as before, is all-powerful still. And yet their deep, infantile need has not been satisfied either, so they seek to make their partner into mother.

Most women do not consciously wish to be their mate's mother but wind up playing out the scenario anyway. It is not hard to see why adult intimate relationships are often troubled, given the primacy of the mother encounter. All our unassimilated need, fear and rage are acted out in intimate relationships. The closer these relationships, the more contaminated they are with the detritus of the primal relationship that the boy *cum* man carries.

Given individual psychological histories, and the consequent intertwining complexities of projection between people, it is a wonder that any relationship can work at all. Sometimes, when a woman becomes mother to the man, it may "work," but at the cost of the psychological liberation of the man from his mother complex (not to mention the fetters retained by the woman). Sexual intimacy is especially freighted with this archaic burden, because having sex is for many men the primal reconnection, the closest they ever feel to the positive mother.

The ghost of the mother may assert itself in the so-called virgin-whore complex, where the man can only be enthusiastically sexual with the "dark" side of the feminine, while he assigns his wife the role of an unapproachable Madonna. Some men are active sexually until their partners become pregnant, or mothers, and then their inner traffic is suddenly too intense. Their eros is sucked down and into the mother complex; they become asexual with their wives, their eros is projected outward in fantasies about other women or acted out in affairs. The romantic Other, for whom one once yearned, is now "domesticated," contaminated with unconscious mother material. The sexual infantility evidenced in men's magazines and beauty pageants is a symptom of the need to place eros on a pedestal, for the world of concrete women demands too much. The playboy is literally a boy at play; he can never be a man until he has wrested his eros from the powerful mother-world within.

Most tragically, men whose eros is still bound up in the mother complex feel the same need, fear and rage toward their own, inner feminine, the anima. To be separated from one's own soul is a terrible wound. One woman said of her husband, "I am his emotional dialysis machine." The child of a cold and critical family, the man had distanced himself from that world of pain. But where was his anima to go? Well, no surprise, it was displaced onto his wife. When he felt angry, and that was unacceptable to him, he provoked *her* to anger and then stood back, judgmentally, at what he had wrought. When he drove her from their bedroom he felt righteous indignation at her abandonment. His emotions, which were in fact precious to him, were just too painfully charged for him to process himself. His wife's metaphor of emotional dialysis was not inexact.

An even worse case was the man who, when his wife would say to him, perhaps once a year, "Charles, we have to talk," would reply, "If you're going to start that again, I'm leaving." This sounds like something out of a *New Yorker* cartoon, but it was a factual expression of the quantum of fear this man carried and experienced in the prospect of opening up a dialogue with his wife.

The greatest cost of the unexamined mother complex, thus, is not the damage it does to outer relationships, though that is often horrendous, but what it does to a man's relationship with himself. What is unconscious does not go away, ever; it is active in the soul. Such self-estrangement erodes the quality of life and poisons relationships. For a man to heal he must first take account of the unresolved, internalized mother-child experience, examine the character of his wounds, both personal and cultural, and, finally, understand the place of the father in this emotional constellation.

3

The Necessary Wounding:
Rites of Passage

While passing through the Shenandoah Valley recently, my wife and I heard the sound of gunfire. Then, surrealistically, we saw batteries of cannon firing and lines of blue and gray arrayed opposite each other. We had happened on an anniversary recreation of the Battle of New Market, where the young cadets of the Virginia Military Institute in nearby Lexington had rushed into battle in May of 1864—the classroom strategies becoming all too real, and, for many, final.

As we watched the exchange of gunfire I felt strangely ambivalent, rather like an obscene tourist at someone else's suffering. I knew there was no surgeon's tent at the rear, no pile of severed limbs, as happens in real battle, no family who would have its heart torn forever, no strips of paper pinned to the back so that one could be identified (having fallen, hopefully, facing the enemy). Though that war had its noble purpose, I could not help but recall the lines of Wilfrid Owen, shortly before he led his platoon to die a week before the armistice in 1918, in which he counsels:

> My friend, you would not tell with such high zest
> To children ardent for some desperate glory,
> The old Lie: Dulce et decorum est
> Pro patria mori.[39]

And the bitter lines by Siegfried Sassoon:

> You smug-faced crowds with kindling eye
> Who cheer when soldier lads march by,
> Sneak home and pray you'll never know
> The hell where youth and laughter go.[40]

---

[39] "Dulce et Decorum Est," in Simon Fuller, ed., *The Poetry of War, 1914-1989*, p. 20.
[40] "Suicide in the Trenches," ibid., p. 21.

I also thought of Gerald, an analysand who as a nineteen year old had found himself in the central highlands of Vietnam. Carrying an M-16 and a radio, he visited places with names like Pleiku and the Ia Drang Valley. He saw one of his buddies cut a peasant in half with his machine gun just for the hell of it. He saw friends with VC ears on a necklace. Then, twenty-four hours after Pleiku, he was in Los Angeles. It took him nearly a year to visit his folks in north Jersey. He just could not go back to the old places and people. And I thought of Hemingway's remark that after the Great War, such terms as *honor* and *duty* had become obscenities and the only sacred words were the names of towns, hills and rivers where men had died.

I had to wonder why any of us were there, that day, at New Market, Virginia. Certainly I did not object to honoring those who died almost 130 years ago. Although I imagine issues of commerce and regional hegemony were more important than the noble desire to end slavery, I suspect many men who took to that field did so because they were even more afraid not to. They were there because they sought the so-called red badge of courage and were more afraid of cowardice and disgrace than showering canisters of shrapnel. Homer knew this. In the *Iliad*, when the Trojan hero Hector is asked why he fought with such valor, he replies that he is more afraid of being shamed by his comrades than of being pierced by Greek lances. Thus is fear the piper that plays the tune to which men dance, and march off to war, unconsciously.

When, as a child during the war years, I discerned a future appointment on some foreign soil, I read all I could about war so that I might ready myself. As a graduate student during Vietnam I received a deferment and a high lottery number; I was relieved but ashamed. I felt I had failed some great test, though I had no conscious illusions about the war, nor any desire to visit Da Nang. I respected those who went, and also those who stayed and protested. I respected conscientious objectors, recalling the words of Karl Shapiro: "Yours is the conscience we came home to."[41] But I also felt shame and won-

---

[41] "Conscientious Objector," in *Modern Verse in English*, p. 574.

dered how I might have measured up. I knew it was no shame to be afraid, but I wondered if, in the face of terror, I could have passed the test and not let my buddies down. Though I have had my share of Tet Offensives since, in confronting the inner demons through the analytic descent into the underworld, I still wonder.

My point here is not to debate matters of war or foreign policy. Rather it is to make clear the Saturnian burden once again. While every civilization must, to preserve itself, make enormous demands on its citizens, each man is wounded by such a summons. Having examined in the previous chapter the enormous influence of the mother complex in a man's life, we must now examine how male wounding is both necessary and, sometimes, appalling.

During the question and response session after a talk I had given to a Jung Society, a man stood up and said, as best I recall: "I am middle-aged now. A few years ago, when I was thirty-eight, my wife told me she didn't love me any more and was leaving me. I was devastated. I wanted to die. Now I realize she did me a favor. I drove her away. She forced me to deal with my anger, my fear of abandonment. She forced me to deal with myself."

While he did not use the word anima, it was clear that the man's wife had forced him to deal with his inner life because she would no longer accept his projections onto her. His wounding was painfully obvious, but his courage, his willingness to work on himself, was the more impressive. His comments bespoke the truth of Nietzsche's aphorism: "What does not destroy us may make us stronger."[42]

So, then, the double-edged sword of wounding. There are wounds that crush the soul, distort and misdirect the energy of life, and those that prompt us to grow up.

One of my first analysands in Zürich was a middle-aged man who had never had a relationship with a woman. He experienced sexual arousal only when he fantasized a woman beating a child or when he could kiss a woman's foot. He had never met his father and his mother had been the leader of a religious commune. Her assaults on

---

[42] "Twilight of the Gods," in *The Portable Nietzsche,* p. 467.

his eros had inflicted terrible wounds, destroying his fragile hold on masculinity.

On the other hand, there are "necessary" wounds, those that quicken consciousness, obliging us to move out of the old dispensation into new life, catalysts to the next stage of growth. As Jung noted, behind one's wound there often lies a person's genius.[43] The ambivalent nature of wounding obliges us, then, to differentiate between those that crush and those that enliven. Again, we are trying to understand with some objectivity what our ancestors often grasped intuitively. Wounding has always been a crucial dimension of male initiation to adulthood, to sacred societies and even sometimes to profession.

Thus another male secret: *because men must leave Mother, and transcend the mother complex, wounding is necessary.*

I have before me the work of the nineteenth-century American painter George Catlin. Trained as a lawyer, the young Catlin crossed the Mississippi and visited some thirty-eight separate Indian nations, often the first white they had seen. He left behind many paintings of their leaders, scenes of the hunt and everyday life, and their rituals. One looks with horror at his paintings of the Mandan Sioux initiatory rites. A skewer was driven into the pectoral muscles of the initiate and he was raised by rope from those hooks toward the ceiling of the ceremonial lodge. He was swung around, hanging from the hooks in his breast, until he fainted. Then he was lowered to the ground and when he recovered he placed a finger on a buffalo skull, the digit to be severed as a further sacrifice.[44]

The history of civilization is full of less dramatic but no less decisive examples of initiation. What are the messages conveyed by such apparent cruelty?

First, as Joseph Campbell notes:

> The boy is being carried across the difficult threshold, from the sphere of dependency on the mothers to that of participation in the

---

[43] "The Gifted Child," *The Development of Personality*, CW 17, par. 244.
[44] Harold McCracken, *George Catlin and the Old Frontier*, pp.106ff.

nature of the fathers, not only by means of a decisive physical transformation of his own body . . . but also by means of a series of intense psychological experiences, reawakening but at the same time
reorganizing all the primary imprints and fantasies of the infantile
unconscious.[45]

Whether the act of ritual mutilation be circumcision, sub-incision,
knocking out a tooth or clipping off an ear or finger, what is sacrificed is material *(mater*-mother) security and dependency. The elders
wrench the boy from his oedipal dependence and cut off the easy re-
liance on the known, the protective, the secure, all aspects of the
mother world.

However painful such ordeals, they were acts of love by the elder
for the younger. They moved from gratuitous acts of violence on
helpless victims to the realm of the religious, since they were at-
tended by the rites of male community, song, dance and the use of
the "bull-roarer" to induce a trance-like state, one transcending the
ordinary. Those swinging by their pectorals from the ridge poles of
the Sioux lodges were, through ceremony and pain, vouchsafed an
ecstatic experience. That is, they were translated from childhood existence in the here and now into the transcendent realm of sacred history, the history of their gods, their people and male mysteries.

Such rites were far more elaborate for boys than for girls. As
Mircea Eliade explains,

> For boys, initiation represents an introduction to a world that is not
> immediate—the world of spirit and culture. For girls, on the con-
> trary, initiation involves a series of revelations concerning the secret
> meaning of a phenomenon that is apparently natural—the visible
> sign of their sexual maturity.[46]

Thus for girls, initiation into adult society meant simply replicating
their mother's world, biologically and phenomenologically experienced with the onset of menstruation. But for boys, the advent of
puberty signaled the move from dependent childhood to the demand-

---

45 *The Masks of God: Primitive Mythology,* p. 99.
46 *Rites and Symbols of Initiation,* p. 47.

ing adult role of keeper and preserver of the symbolic values of the tribe. These values included honoring the directives of the gods, membership in the collective, and keeping watch on the ramparts.

The move from the creature comforts of the hearth to the frontier, from body and instinct to symbolic service, from childhood to adulthood, requires the crossing of a huge psychological divide. The wounding rites, then, are inflicted ritually, bestowed with eros, to help both the youth and the society he must sustain. As he encounters pain, with all its immediacy, he learns in the rigors of his flesh the message that he can't go home again. He is granted an ecstatic vision, crosses that divide and enters the adult world. How difficult it is for men today who have no help across that great abyss. There are no rites, very few wise elders, and minimal modeling of mature male initiates. So most of us are left to our private dependencies, to swaggering about in embarrassing macho compensation, or, most commonly, to suffering our shame and indecision in isolation.

Given the similarity of structure, sequence and motive in the rites of passage among disparate and geographically separate cultures, one would have thought their ceremonies ordained by some central committee. Barring that impossibility, it would seem that such ceremonies originated spontaneously, that is, welled up from archetypal roots. Most mythic motifs and transcendent visions originate in the psychic life of the individual or of the small group. These images arise to support and direct the flow of libido, to channel human energy in meaningful ways. So, then, we might expect that the work of our own depths, our unconscious processes, might also incarnate passages, for in each man's psyche course the same energies that animated our ancestors.

Such a summons to manhood may be seen in the dream of twenty-eight-year-old Norman. Norman recalled only one good time in his life. That was when, having abused drugs and dropped out of college, he moved in with an uncle and worked side by side with him in a bakery. But the gravitational pull of his family colluded with his lack of confidence to bring him back to live with his parents. For several years he drifted in and out of psychiatric treatment, though he had no significant pathological features. His problems were rather developmental, that is, problems of maturation and separation. His mother was psychologically invasive, his father absent on business most of the time and extremely passive even when present.

When Norman came to me I suggested he move out of the parental home to at least launch the first step of the initiation process—physical separation. His mother phoned me, upset, and said, "But you're not thinking like a mother." "No, Ma'am," I replied, "I'm thinking like his therapist." (I might have said "like a tribal elder," but I doubt that would have made sense to her.)

While in analysis Norman continued to vacillate between a dependency that frequently drove him home or to telephone his mother, and a rageful enervation that followed each contact with her. One might say that his soul was up for grabs. It would be easy enough to blame his unconscious mother, for she certainly baited traps for him, or his passive father, who provided no model of initiation. But that would be to undermine Norman's personal responsibility and task: to hold the tension between his desire to become an adult and his fear of independence. This tremendous struggle, this daily vacillation, was dramatized in a very powerful three-part dream:

> I am at a drive-in movie with male friends. Something has happened to the car and I get out to investigate. Someone hits me very hard in the mouth.
>
> I am with my mother looking in the mirror together. She expresses her sympathy. My tooth falls out. It can't be saved. I go over and show the tooth to Keith Byars.[47]
>
> I find Mrs. X. I say to her, "I am not a little boy. Treat me like a man."

The dream says it all. It shows Norman stuck in the no-man's-land of extended adolescence.[48] The setting announces his situation

---

[47] Keith Byars was a highly-regarded running back for the Philadelphia Eagles, Norman's favorite football team, at the time of the dream.

[48] Many in the helping professions currently define adolescence as between the ages of twelve and twenty-eight, given the absence of rites of passage to adulthood. Norman was clearly pushing even these liberal limits.

in life. The movie theater suggests a projected interior drama where he is working with the masculine presence; however, there is a problem with the car, his psychic process or mobility. When he makes a move he is wounded. Before he began therapy Norman knew nothing of male rites of passage, but his psyche, at the archetypal level, knows, for it participates in the primal developmental process. He did not consciously know that ritual wounding, sometimes in fact the knocking out of a tooth, was symbolic of sacrificing dependence on the mother. While Norman's mother made it difficult for him to separate, his own lethargy stymied his growth as well. In the dream he seeks her sympathy, her commiseration—"poor baby." At the same time his split psyche moves to show "Keith Byars" the tooth, which is to say that in his personal and collective culture, his psyche fastened on this athlete as a personification of male energy that might help combat the chthonic pull of the underworld.

Norman's father is not present in the mirroring, but the football player represents a male energy for which he longs and whose affirmation he needs. Ambivalence dominates, however, for in the third part of the dream Norman seeks the support of Mrs. X (a neighbor whom Norman believed to be more understanding and supportive than his mother). Thus the dream does not represent a breakthrough. At the end Norman is still soliciting an older woman's approval.

This regressive force is found in all men, but here the pathology arises from the near complete absence of positive male energy in Norman's history. When such energy is present it helps model and counterbalance the regressive pull of the mother complex. One sees why Norman considered the brief shoulder-to-shoulder stint with his uncle as the best time of his life. Yet even that glimpse of maturity was overcome by the powerful energies of the complex and his own failure of nerve.[49]

---

[49] In Grimm's "Iron Hans" fairy tale, the key to the wild man lies under the mother's pillow. The youth cannot ask her for the key, for she will not give it. She wishes him to remain by her side. And so it must be stolen in order to unlock the energies of adulthood. (See below, pp. 92-94, for further consideration of "Iron Hans.")

In the absence of rites of passage, in the absence of tribal elders, Norman's plight is common to many men today. They are expected to grow up, know themselves, serve and maintain the tribal culture, and be comfortable with their identity. An older male therapist may help somewhat to provide support and encouragement, but weekly sessions are hardly enough and, in any case, lack the numinosity of traditional initiation rites.[50] Norman, for instance, did eventually spend less and less time with his parents, slowly growing less dominated by them and his parental complexes. He now lives separately and supports himself. But psychologically he has remained, essentially, the uninitiated, wounded male characteristic of our time.

Norman's missing tooth in the dream is symbolic of the sacrifice of creature comforts and a summons to the rigors of the journey. This sacrifice is a most powerful mythological motif, an archetypal pattern which requires that something be given up for something to be gained. Childhood dependency must be relinquished for adult self-possession and creativity. The longing for a trouble-free existence must be put aside in favor of the mature meeting of responsibility. Such changes constitute not only the quickening of consciousness but a form of election. All are summoned to grow up; not all are up to the task. Initiatory wounding is an adumbration of things to come—the wounding ways of the world. When the child goes off to kindergarten he not only mourns the loss of the protective hearth, he also intuits the existence of a more difficult and dangerous world. As natural as it is to fear that world, he is obliged to enter it if he is to claim his own adulthood.

When I was an adolescent, and against parental advice, I played football in high school and college. On the first day of practice I had a fingernail torn off. As I stood on the sideline and commiserated with myself, a senior tackle came over and said, to the best of my recollection, "If you can't stand that, you won't stand the rest. It gets worse." I felt at that moment a kind of male love, a friendly encour-

---

[50] As constructive and supportive as therapy may be, it does not involve ritual burial and rebirth, or swinging from the pectorals. No ecstatic vision, only talk. Such talk is necessary, and healing, but it also takes longer.

agement. He could easily have shamed me, as men often do to each other, but his tone suggested helpfulness and I internalized it as encouragement. Even though I was rather small for organized football, I felt a deep drive to play. I could not have expressed why.

In retrospect, the motives come easily to mind. I was afraid of getting hurt by the bigger guys. I overcompensated for that dread by entering the field of fear by choice. Each Friday I would be doubled over in abdominal pain from that fear, but I never missed a practice or a game. Like the Trojan Hector, I was more afraid of being afraid than getting hurt. When, at the end of my first year, I broke my thumb, I felt a symbolic victory, a red badge of courage, no less. Unconsciously, I was seeking male bonding—to knock heads with the guys, joke with them, cry together when we lost. My psyche drew me to sweat, collision and fear as a rite of passage. What my parents could not understand, nor did I at the time, was that football was all that was available to me in a mythically sterile time. In the need for symbolic wounding, for association with male energy and camaraderie, and for a rite of passage from childhood and the encapsulation of the mother complex, all I had was football.

Just a few years ago I woke up having dreamt of my old college football coach. I had not seen him for thirty years. Finding his address in the alumni journal, I wrote to him in Indianapolis. He remembered me and in recounting his life since added, "That's what we learned from football. You get hurt and you get up and get ready for the next play." Maybe this is a simplistic message for life, but it surely is a necessary one. Perhaps my psyche dredged him up after all those years to remind me of that message.

One recent Labor Day my wife and I set off to walk our dog. It was very early and the high school field across the way was still shrouded with mist. We could see dim forms in the distance and hear the faint cadence chant. My wife said how awful it was that the coach had the boys out there on a holiday rather than letting them be home with their families. I replied that they wanted to be there, that they had fought for the privilege. I did not add that they also wanted to be hurt, somehow, in the daily collisions, that they needed each other, that it was about love somehow, and that they were looking for their fathers there in the mist. I did not add all that for I did not believe I would be able to make it clear. Indeed, not until I had confronted the inner dragons in my own analysis did I realize that I had never done anything wiser or more necessary than go out on a green field of play and break my thumb.

On such fields what the youth is seeking, though he knows it not, is the forgotten rite of passage and the lost fathers. He is seeking, in Jung's terms, the symbolic life. Meaning only comes to us "when people feel that they are living the symbolic life, that they are actors in the divine drama."[51] The youth is seeking, in however culturally attenuated a form, images that will attract his libido and channel it to serve his development and his community. His need to individuate is profound and has an archetypal urgency. Without such images and rites he is bereft. He will spend his time in depression, or take drugs to kill the pain. Like Norman, he will stay suspended as a child-man, or engage in macho overcompensation. He will believe that his masculinity is proved by bedding women, driving a high-powered car or making lots of money. Underneath he knows the truth, of course, and he is desperately afraid of being found out; he believes himself an impostor in the company of men.

Those same trials on fields of green are experienced by all men in many different forums. No man I have ever met, if he is honest enough to admit it, has not felt a great deal of shaming as a man. The same salubrious power of wounds to stir growth can also damage a man's sense of self. No male client with whom I have ever worked has not at some time felt inadequate or shamed. Most had vivid memories of failure, like the time they dropped the ball and lost the game, or when they failed to make the team. For boys, such green fields and their analogue, dusty playgrounds, are the arena for testing and for shaming.

What man does not remember the slogans on the locker room walls? "No pain. No gain." "When the going gets tough, the tough

---

[51] See above, note 12.

get going." Who does not remember childhood games of rough and tumble? One man who had led a very distinguished, high-profile career always referred to what he called "The Red Surrender." When he was around nine years old a bigger kid named Red had held him down on the playground and heaped dirt on his face while the others laughed. No matter how great his achievements in the adult world, "The Red Surrender" remained his mythically defining moment. What man does not recall being called a "sissy," or, worse when I was a child, a "jelly"? These wounds are permanently lodged in a man's psyche and much of his adult life may be spent jousting with the armored ghosts of humiliations past.

Alas, he may not speak of this shame, this humiliation, lest he be shamed further. And this is the fourth great secret men carry: *they collude in a conspiracy of silence whose aim is to suppress their emotional truth.*

Every man will recall times when, as a boy, as a youth, or even last week, he dared reveal himself and was shamed and isolated. He learns to stuff that shame, mask it in male bravado and cover, cover, cover. Along the way he is frequently degraded and unable to speak his pain, his protest. The play, and later film, *Glengarry Glen Ross,* dramatizes the humiliation of the sales force of a real-estate company, fully grown men abusing their male colleagues who suffer and turn the other cheek while trying to beat each other at the selling game: to the top salesman a Cadillac, to the second a paltry set of steak knives, and the fourth was to be unemployed. In such ways is shame swallowed and isolation deepened. The shaming and the secrecy have gone on since childhood, so men become accomplices in their own degradation. This keeps them from embracing either their broken brothers or their own splintered selves.

Men are often amazed by the willingness of women to share their pain. Even as a therapist I have been impressed by women's capacity to gain access to their inner truth and articulate it to another. Jungian therapist Robert Hopcke goes so far as to say that in his experience it takes men a year in therapy to reach the point where women usually begin, in terms of being able to express what they are really feeling.[52] Men will express their frustration or speak of a problem "out there," but they are seldom able to articulate the reality of their inner world. Such is the legacy of the shaming and self-alienation they have accrued since childhood.

Two examples will suffice. One is the man who came to see me at the express demand of his wife and condescendingly noted the presence of a box of tissues.[53] They served to remind him of the lake of tears within himself, and his old defenses were quickly activated. Predictably, he lasted about three sessions in therapy, and his marriage only two months longer. I found myself quick to judge him, but upon reflection I felt sorry for him. His maleness was so wounded that he had to clothe himself in a macho cloak. He was a terribly isolated man. The innocuous box of tissue served as a spark for all the shame and risk and fear he had suffered. As a consequence of his self-alienation he could hardly have a safe and trusting relationship with his wife. Instead he sought to control her.

On another occasion, while counseling a policeman and his wife, I felt genuine sympathy for his description of how much he worried about money. At the same time he described how he daily had to deal with "the scum of the earth." He was very much the battered, wounded male of whom I have been speaking. His wounds seemed only to crush his spirit, not free him for new consciousness. Several times he had lashed out at his wife, hitting her once, and feared he might do the same to his daughter. At one point in the session he got up and came straight at me to make a point; I think if I had moved he would have hit me. The battered man, with his battered inner child, can only batter others because he cannot bear to speak his pain.

The willingness of women to risk their inner truth, which men generally lack, means that women are much less likely to feel alienated. In my experience, women adjust to divorce or the loss of a spouse far better than do men. Perhaps they feel less abandoned because they have learned along the way to establish a relationship with

---

52 *Men's Dreams, Men's Healing*, p. 12.
53 See above, pp. 43-44.

their own inner life. Certainly they are more likely to have a supportive network of friends. After divorce or a partner's death, a man is
far more likely to neglect his health and become depressed, sitting in
a dark room with a bottle and a TV dinner. And he is more likely to
rush out and find a replacement as soon as possible, just to avoid the
loneliness.

Men's mortality rate shoots up shortly after retirement, apparently
because their immune system is depressed. Perhaps also the Saturnian wound, that a man is to be judged by his productivity, occasions a great lost of self-esteem. All his life he has been told he *is* his
work. If he stopped working, or supporting those whom he is
obliged to support, he would be shamed and shunned. He would be
a lazy bum, irresponsible. St. Niklaus, who left his family, became
the patron saint of Switzerland; the French painter Paul Gauguin
abandoned wife and kids to make his mark in Fiji; but few can pull it
off. As a wage-slave a man may be degraded, but he will accept that
before being shamed as nonproducing.

Our culture offers a delusory out: "At 65, or thereabouts, you no
longer have to work to prove your worth. Now you can retire honorably from the field and, without any preparation of your soul along
the way, you can play out your days at shuffleboard in Sun City or
St. Petersburg." Fueled by economic need, and even more by the
fear of shameful inadequacy, we are all, in the haunting words of
Philip Larkin,

> men whose first coronary is coming like Christmas—who drift,
> loaded helplessly with commitments and obligations and necessary
> observances, into the darkening avenues of age and incapacity, de-
> serted by everything that once made life sweet.

What the modern man most suffers from, then, is the wounding
without the transformation. He suffers the Saturnian burden of role
definition that confines rather than liberates. He suffers the skewers
in the soul without the godly vision. He is asked to be a man when
no one can define it except in the most trivial of terms. He is asked to
move from boyhood to manhood without any rites of passage, with

no wise elders to receive and instruct him, and no positive sense of what such manhood might feel like. His wounds are not transformative; they do not bring deepened consciousness; they do not lead him to a richer life. They senselessly, repeatedly, stun him into a numbing of the soul before the body has had the good sense to die.

Richard is a lawyer in a large firm. He dreams that a man confronts Arnold Schwartzenegger, pulls the skin off his face and puts it on himself. Richard feels humiliated in the dream. His association with the image is the fear that his colleagues at work do not respect him, that he may not be pulling his weight. Similarly, he dreams that he and his wife are asleep when an intruder enters. Richard is frozen in terror and thinks, "I'll have to get up and defend our house." He shouts, "Get out of here!" A year later he dreams of another intruder, who this time moves toward his daughter's room. Richard gets up and goes after the intruder with a baseball bat.

Richard's understanding of these recurrent dream images is that his role in life is to provide for and protect his family. He feels afraid, inadequate, not fully a man. He confessed these thoughts to a therapist only because the dreams were so insistent. In another dream he sees someone beating someone else. He yells, "Leave him alone." The assailant chases him. "We fight. I kick him in the balls. I hit him and he is dazed, but he gets control of me and torments me. Then he takes my shoes. No one can help me." Again, Richard feels unable to defend himself and those in his care. His tormentor steals his shoes, his grounding, his standpoint.

Or consider Allen, an emergency room physician. He dreams he is in a room with other youngish men. All of them are successfully shooting arrows. He has to do this too, but no one will show him how or what to shoot at. Finally he does shoot his arrows, but he has no sense of whether they have hit the target or not. Then the scene shifts and he is in a swamp crawling with alligators. He wrestles with one that is trying to pull him under. Full of terror, he manages to escape and reach a mud flat where he will be safe for a moment. Apparently Allen's psyche longs for a rite of passage. He sees that other young men are already engaged, but there is no elder to instruct. He does not even know what the target is or whether his halting efforts are rightly directed. As a consequence he is swamped, a powerful symbol of the undertow of the unconscious. Without the helpful father, the dreamer is in the death grip of the maternal monster, his mother complex, which threatens to pull him under. Though he clambers onto a mud flat, he is only temporarily safe.

Notice that these two men are in professions that culturally endow them with considerable empowerment. Yet both feel unworthy and fearful of tests of their manhood. They long for the help of others over the great divide; they suffer wounds without illumination or transformation. The absence of meaningful rites of passage to manhood haunts their dreams, just as it does those of so many men. Again, only by fidelity to the inner life, for instance by treating their dreams with respect, however unpleasant the message, will they be able to bring their secret fears to the light of consciousness.

As a consequence of missing rites of passage, men doubt their masculinity. They feel that however tightly they have been able to circle the wagons, someone will break through and humiliate, even destroy them. Or, life will shift the context, change the game, and one will be proven incompetent. So the double bind is: be a man and prove it, but the rules shift constantly so you don't even know how to play the game. And once you have "arrived," the rules will change again and someone else will be better than you. This protean, shape-changing definition of masculinity obliges men to function at the persona level, defining their reality primarily in terms of collective parameters such as salary, car, home, social status.

The fragile psyche of man has been brutalized and trivialized. Historically he has been conditioned to procreate and protect his brood, and to be defined by his productivity. All that says little or nothing about his soul, his personhood, his uniqueness. In such a world men are tragically doomed; they cannot achieve serenity, seldom operate out of inner conviction, and rarely get out of the killing game. Even when they win, they lose their soul.

Thus modern men recapitulate the timeless lineaments of an ancient myth, that of the wounded Fisher King, Amfortas. The tale of

Amfortas, whose name derives from French *enfertez*, "infirmity," has been told many, many times, from various versions of the medieval Grail legend to Robert Johnson's modern account in *He: Understanding Male Psychology*. The central point is that Amfortas has suffered a terrible wound, variously described as to the thigh or the testicles. He has been wounded in his place of generativity, the seat of his maleness. It is a wound that will not heal unless he find the Grail, medieval symbol for container of soul. Though modern man may have a big car in the castle garage and walls adorned with the trophies of corporate success, he intuits his emptiness, his pain, the wound that will not heal. However magnificent the castle he has created and the ramparts on which he nervously strides, he knows he is the lord of emptiness, his realm an emotional wasteland.

This recurrent mythic motif hovers in the background of T.S. Eliot's great twentieth-century poem, "The Wasteland." London, the center of commerce and man-built structures, the center of the game, is dubbed an

> Unreal City,
> Under the brown fog of a winter dawn,
> A crowd flowed over London Bridge, so many.
> I had not thought death had undone so many.[54]

At rush hour Eliot sees not the enterprise of life but spiritual death. Thus he ironically quotes Dante's shocked sentence as he walked into the Inferno six centuries before ("I had not thought death had undone so many"). If the world men have made and serve does not serve them, then they are among the hosts of the dead in the wasteland of the soul. As Joseph Campbell explained it,

> The Wasteland . . . is any world in which . . . force and not love, indoctrination, not education, authority, not experience, prevail in the ordering of lives, and where myths and rites enforced and received are consequently unrelated to the actual inward realizations, needs, and potentialities of those upon whom they are impressed.[55]

---

54 "The Wasteland," lines 60-63, in *The Complete Poems and Plays*, p. 39.
55 *The Masks of God: Creative Mythology*, p. 388.

When outer myth and inner truth conflict, one suffers a wound of the soul. Men surely suspect that attaining material success and power-laden status will not bring them inner peace, but they are afraid to get out of what is, as far as they know, the only game in town. So the wound festers without new vision, without healing.

In a short story Delmore Schwartz describes a young man who, on the morn of his twenty-first birthday, dream he is in a theater. To his amazement he sees his parents meeting and courting on the silver screen. As he watches the film he realizes they are making a terrible mistake, a mistake from which he, of course, will one day result. He stands up and shouts that the film must be stopped. He is accosted by the usher who admonishes him firmly, "You can't act like this even if other people aren't around! You will be sorry if you do not do what you should do, you can't carry on like this, you will find that out soon enough."[56]

Thus the youth, at the onset of his chronological adulthood, sees the burden of the family mythos that will shape him. Rejecting his parents before his birth, he rejects the life awaiting him as their child. And just so do many men carry a secret sorrow and rage that the familial and cultural ethos, the images and expectations that hammer them into shape, are not in accord with the truth in their soul.

The collision between outer images and inner truth creates an impossible dilemma for men. The man in the gray flannel suit, the organization man, the team player—all represent enormous pressures to conform, to distort the soul, even as that of women has so often been. This collision, felt in body and spirit if not also in the conscious mind, leads to another male truth that is rather less than a secret: *Men's lives are violent because their souls have been violated.*

Men's violence breaks out in random acts of murder and rape, and in psychic contagions such as mob action and wars. Dig deeply into any man and one will quickly find not only that lake of tears but a mountain of rage, layers of anger accumulated since childhood, slowly pushing its magma toward the surface, there to erupt.

---

[56] "In Dreams Begin Responsibilities," in *The World Is a Wedding.*

I once sat with a man who had taken over his father's plumbing business when the elder's health declined. He worked sixty hours a week for forty years, protected his parents and allowed them to die in some modicum of material comfort. Then he protected his two sons from the Saturnian rack where, in Gerard Manley Hopkins's words, "All is seared with trade; bleared, smeared with toil; / and wears man's smudge and shares man's smell."[57] The sons, protected thus, remained at home, dependent and demanding. At the slightest provocation he would erupt and scream at his poor wife, storm and threaten. His rage was the anger accumulated from a life lost, given to others, given to Saturn. And yet he had obeyed sacrosanct cultural values: take care of your parents, provide for your family, pass on a better life to your children. He did everything he was supposed to do except live his own life, and he was full of rage.

Another man I knew had devoted his life to the making of international peace. He was a widely traveled negotiator, director of a respected think tank on conflict resolution. I never saw him angry and he never raised his voice. At first I was perplexed at where his anger was. Then he told me that at least once a month he was wiped out by migraines. His legitimate, honest anger turned inward. He attacked the only person his fine sensibility would allow—himself.

One Monday morning at rush hour, along with other commuters, I ground to a halt in the Philadelphia traffic—a gridlock from which no one would move very soon. At the intersection two men got out of expensive cars, and, clad in suits and ties, screamed at each other and shook their fists. I suspect that their accumulated rage at life, not to mention what lay in wait at their respective offices, had been tapped and burst forth.

Similarly, I am always on edge while attending Philadelphia Eagle football games. In the parking lots, and in the cheaper seats especially, the passerby's life is in danger. So many men, fueled by brew and pot, fight each other or anyone in their way. At one game my daughter and I counted sixteen fights in our section of the stadium.

---

[57] "God's Grandeur," lines 6-7, in *Norton Anthology of Poetry,* p. 855.

On another occasion my wife and I were threatened directly because we had allegedly parked our car too close to the van of some yahoos who had started their bread and wine before the game. Another time an elderly man who had dressed as a native American during an Eagles-Redskins game was beaten up inside and again later outside the stadium. For some reason he expressed no desire to visit the City of Brotherly Love again.

What do these examples illustrate? For the young football fans the week before the game is a Saturnian round of boring and oppressive jobs, low pay, little expectation of change, a circus-like setting of stylized violence, and the ministrations of booze—a witch's brew for the venting of anger. They are angry at the roles they seem doomed to play out. They are angry at women because of their unconscious mother complex. Each is angry at being a man, and, unconsciously, acts out his rage—

> climbs the building, kicks the football, boxes his brother in the hate-ridden city.
> . . . . Howls in his sleep because the tight-rope Trembles and shows the darkness beneath.
> The strutting show-off is terrified.[58]

These working-class lads will likely remain trapped forever within the Saturnian wheel of fate. They will beat their women, drink to mask their pain, suspect each other, ever isolated and afraid. Their more educated or privileged brothers will be successful by societal parameters. But they too, in their leased limos, their Brooks Brothers suits, their executive suites, will have succumbed to the infantility of power, the only game they know.

Since their rage is monumental, and since they cannot speak it truthfully lest they be shamed, most modern men drift further into isolation. Accordingly, they turn their rage on themselves. They do drugs, drink too much or work out until they drop. They must reach a place where they feel no pain, where they can slow down. Many of

---

[58] Delmore Schwartz, "The Heavy Bear," in *Modern Poems: An Introduction to Poetry,* pp. 309-310.

them are workaholics; work keeps them from confronting the demands of their anima. Work drains and fatigues them till they can honorably fall into bed exhausted. You don't have to be a therapist to know that anger turned inward may somatize or become depression. Since stress is measurable, much of popular psychology usefully, if superficially, teaches stress management. Heart and blood pressure and stomach and headache pathologies are the children of stress. Is not a shorter life span also pathological?

Think of those nifty beer commercials, put together by some pretty smart guys, showing men laboring together at logging camp or high in a skyscraper. Then, "It's Miller time by Bud's early Lite!" and they're off to the local watering hole, to "happy hour," where with a blond or brunette anima they can afford to feel what was not felt that day. What a happy band of brothers—secure, free and supported by male community—in the alcohol paradise envisioned by ad agencies. The truth is that they too are men "whose first coronary is coming like Christmas." Their hearts have been under attack long before the cardiac arrests to which Philip Larkin's poem alludes. Theirs is the loneliness of the long-distance runner.

The Saturnian rack turns. Every man is on it. Their wounds do not quicken consciousness or bring wisdom. They merely cause pain without meaning. The anesthetic of work, the numbing of narcotics, be they chemical or ideological, the terror of loneliness—all wounds without transformation. Such wounds are barbarous, soul-less.

Yes, it is necessary that men be wounded to help them break free from the Mother. But it is necessary also that those wounds further growth. Today's man suffers his wounds in isolation, but his reaction troubles and damages those around him. He must begin by acknowledging the wounds he carries, wounds that leak daily into his life, if ever he is to heal himself or help his world.

4

Father Hunger

All imagos are two-sided. If an image has a depth dimension it must express the dual character of reality. Acknowledging and maintaining the tension of opposites is a fundamental Jungian tenet. One-sidedness begets distortion, perversion, neurosis. Thus, for example, the archetype of the mother expresses the dual aspect of nature, that which giveth and that which taketh away. The Great Mother represents a life force that both begets and destroys, gestates and annihilates. As Dylan Thomas so succinctly put it, "The force that through the green fuse drives the flower . . . is my destroyer."[59]

So, too, the archetype of the father is dual. Father gives life, light, energy—no wonder he has historically been associated with the sun. But father can also blast, wither, crush. The preliterate mind, playing with the image of the sun as center of energy, the vitalizing principle, evolved God the Father who energizes and fecundates the feminine earth. Patriarchy replaced the worship of Earth Mother with that of Sky Father. (The halo associated with Christ is a relic of the solar aura of the Father even as the serpent associated with the maternal deities is spurned by the emergent patriarchy in Genesis.) When the experience of the father is positive, the child experiences strength, support, the energizing of his own resources and modeling in the outer world. When the experience of the father is negative, the fragile psyche is crushed.

To use a modern metaphor, the child's psyche is a set of potentialities, a data base to be shaped by the affirmation and modeling of the parents. Through his mother he may experience the world as a nurturing and protective environment. From father he may receive the empowerment to enter the world and to fight for his life. Of course

---

[59] "The Force That Through the Green Fuse," in *Norton Anthology of Poetry*, p. 1176.

mother can help empower him and father nurture him, but archety-
pally they play specific roles. Mother also activates the mother complex, which must be transformed and transcended lest he remain
childlike and dependent. He must leave the world of the mother and
enter that of the fathers. All mythology is a playing out of some vari-
ant of two great mythologems. The mythology of the Great Mother is
the great circle, the death-rebirth motif, the Eternal Return. The
mythology of the Sky Father is the quest, the journey from innocence to experience, from dark to light, from home to the horizon.
Each mythic cycle must be served.

When the parental imagos in the child are inadequately modeled by
the parents, he carries the deficit throughout his life. He longs for
something missing, even as he might carry a vitamin deficiency and
crave a certain food. He unconsciously seeks the dormant energies of
his psyche through others. He may impose the nurturant role on his
wife, for example, and be angry when she does not mother him even
though consciously he would not let her. Or he may relinquish his
own private journey to serve another man's, unconsciously seeking
the missing father imago. He may be full of rage for the failure of his
father to father, or for the absence of cultural fathers, or he may carry
a secret grief for his lost father.

Just as we spent considerable time looking at the power of the
mother complex in a man's life two chapters ago, so we must acknowledge that such power is rendered even greater by the incom-
pletely activated father imago. What the personal father must be,
among other things, is the third point in the triangle of parents and
child. If he is missing, literally or psychologically, the mother's
power will be unbalanced. Or if, unduly influenced by his own
mother complex, the father acts in a brutal, repressive fashion as the
familial power broker, he similarly fails to model a healthy rapprochement with the feminine that the child needs to witness. The old
father-knows-best family model was too one-sided to be healthy.
Few of us grew up seeing our parents as equal agents, democratic
forces balancing, supporting, complementing each other.

In *Finding Our Fathers,* Sam Osherson cites a broad study indicating that only seventeen per cent of American men had a positive relationship with their fathers. In most cases the father was dead, divorced and missing, chemically impaired or emotionally absent.[60] If this amazing statistic is even close to the truth, something large and tragic has happened to one of the critical balances of nature. Indeed, Robert Bly asserts that the father-son relationship is the most damaged of all relationships since the industrial revolution.[61]

Thus the seventh great secret that bedevils the male soul: *each man carries a deep longing for his father and for his tribal fathers.*

When fathers and sons stopped working together in the fields, in the small trades, when the family left the land and migrated to the cities where the jobs were, when father left home and went to the factory and the office, the son was left behind. No more the shared toil, no more the transmission of one's craft, no more the bonding of a boy with his dad. Father dragged himself home from a brutalizing day in the heat of the assembly line or the paper shuffling of the office. Perhaps he had a few on the way home. James Joyce tells the story of a father who, having been trashed by his boss, scorned by his friends, rejected by a woman, walks in the house and, "for no reason," beats his son. The degradation of his soul that day is visited on the only one over whom he still has power.[62]

Fathers so often return home dispirited and soul-worn. They can hardly model a positive masculine imago for their sons when they feel the Saturnian oppression so keenly. There is no point in a man blaming his father, for his father could then blame his father. The chain of cause and effect reaches back to the beginnings of industrial and urban man. When the tribe was absorbed into the larger society, the chance for man-to-man transmissions was virtually lost. We can scarcely go back to tribalism, although one feature of the men's movement has been to try to recapture a sense of it by drumming and chanting, and by bringing men together to share their stories.

---

[60] *Finding Our Fathers*, p. 18.
[61] *Iron John: A Book About Men.* pp. 19ff.
[62] "Counterparts," in *The Portable James Joyce*, pp. 97-109.

Certainly the idea of activating a positive masculine imago is appropriate and male bonding experiences do further that goal. But most men will never be exposed to such opportunities, and, for many who are, the effect of the group experience does not last. What father cannot access in himself cannot be passed on to his son. And we cannot look to corporate boardrooms or the church for the tribal fathers today. So all men, whether they know it or not, hunger for their father and grieve over his loss. They long for his body, his strength, his wisdom.

Literature is full of illustrations of the search that transpires within the youth for the activation of the masculine principle. A fine example is Franz Kafka's short story "The Judgment,"[63] where the personal father complex is extended to include his ambivalence toward the patriarchs of his Judaic heritage and even to Yahweh—stern and demanding, as well as absent and unavailable.

In the story a young man suffers under the omniscient eye of his father. He has secretly been writing to a male friend in Russia. (For the Prague-born Kafka, Russia, at the beginning of this century, would have represented something akin to our nineteenth-century "wild west," a land of frontier adventure.) The friend is urging the youth to join him. Obviously the youth longs for adventure and is eager to accept the summons to journey from home to horizon. But his father finds the cache of letters. He says to the son, "I sentence you to die." The son dutifully treks through the city, crosses a bridge, and, at story's end, jumps to his death in the river.

This denouement shocks the reader. But Kafka, whom W.H. Auden said stands in relationship to our age as Dante did to his,[64] is an unparalleled writer of parables. Kafka's stories are letters to his secret self, penned in an effort to escape an iron father and stultifying tradition, though death seems the only escape from the grim, gray city of oppression. By what power, what authority, even what motive, can the father exercise such an effect over his son? Just as a

---

[63] In *The Penal Colony*, pp. 49-66.
[64] *The Dyer's Hand*, p. 159.

glance at Medusa's face would turn men to stone in classical mythology, so we have in "The Judgment" a portrayal of the power of the negative father complex. This Saturnian shadow has the capacity to fall over a son's spirit and crush him. The son reaches out for a positive masculine experience with his friend, but, for reasons not explained, the father tumbles to his rival and shuts off his son's only hope of escape. The complex, then, has the power to cut off his spirit, to tamp the fires of life and plunge him into the obliterating waters of the unconscious. So, instead of bringing his son light, the father brings suffocating darkness.

Such negative fathers built what Blake called the "dark, satanic mills."[65] They also built Auschwitz. They built arrogant theologies that burned men at the stake and crushed them on the wheel. They have created an iron world without light, without soul. When their sons reach out for life they crush and destroy them.

Quite another example of the quest for the father may be seen in Nathaniel Hawthorne's story, "My Kinsman, Major Molineaux." A youth named Robin sets off to find fame and fortune in Boston, assisted he hopes by his kinsman Major Molineaux, whom he must find. Naive and innocent, he gets lost in the city whose winding streets are a maze, like the convolutions of his own psyche. Everywhere he goes he asks for his kinsman and is surprised to see Bostonians pull back from him. He does not know that the Revolution is brewing and his kinsman is a much-hated royalist official. As night falls his confidence and his consciousness diminish also. He is swept up into a passing mob of men painted as savages. Soon he is howling in their midst. Only then does he realize that he has found his kinsman, tarred and feathered, no helping father but a broken old man. Robin is stunned at finding the violence of the mob in himself and realizes he must make his own way in the world.

Hawthorne's story typifies a young man's need for a father figure, a mentor who will help him over the bridge from his mother complex to the empowered male world beyond. But, like most

[65] "And Did Those Feet," in *Norton Anthology of Poetry,* p. 510.

modern men, Robin does not find the mentor he needs. He finds only a wounded man like others, and a darkness within himself which thereafter he must carry consciously. We might recall the massive shadow projection that fell onto Hitler in the thirties. The Hitler *Jugend* was filled with youths who longed for the activation of their inner hero. They responded to the summons to ideals, sacrifice and communal identification. The appeal of John Kennedy to youthful idealism and heroic need is a more benign example. What Robin found was that there were no helpful fathers, only the *abaissement du niveau mentale* of the mob. In the end he is on his own.

A more positive outcome of the quest for a helpful male companion is seen in Joseph Conrad's novella *The Secret Sharer.* The protagonist is a young captain taking on his first command in the South China Sea. Nervous and insecure, he tries to befriend his crew who immediately smell his fear and belittle him behind his back. He knows only to be friend or tyrant, both extremes undermining his power to command. While walking the deck one night he sees a man in the surf and pulls him aboard. Instinctively he knows he must harbor and protect this man. Later a ship pulls alongside, searching for a man who has acted boldly but murdered a shipmate. The young captain, despite his duty to serve and support the law of the sea, covers for his mysterious visitor.

The man he fished from the sea seems to have all the qualities the young captain lacks. He is in fact his shadow, his *Doppelganqer* or double. At story's end the young captain, having assimilated the psychic influence of the fugitive, puts his ship through some complicated and perilous maneuvers in order to put the man safely ashore. Out of these actions the crew comes to respect the young captain, for he has obviously grasped and now models the requisite moral authority necessary to exercise command.

What the young captain needed was not knowledge—he had already learned that at the naval academy—but inner strength, inner authority. What the mysterious visitor represented was his own shadow potential. They shared a secret, the secret that outer authority must spring from inner authority. This secret sharing is the mentoring all men need. Since they are seldom able to feel their inner authority, men must spend their lives deferring to others or throwing their outer weight around in compensation for their sense of inner weakness. Unlike the Kafka story, where the negative father crushes the child's spirit, or Hawthorne's where the mentor disappoints, Conrad's story illustrates positive mentoring.

All sons need something from their fathers. They especially need their father to say he loves and accepts them as they are.[66] Too many men have distorted their individuation journey because their father did not affirm them. The sons naturally thought they must adjust themselves, twist their nature, to win his approval. Often they win approval by trying to fulfill the father's expectations. Sometimes they spend their life seeking that approval from others. Or, lacking the father's affirmation, they internalize this deficit as a phenomenological statement about themselves. ("If I were worthy, I would have his love. Since I do not, I am unworthy.")

I recall one man in his late thirties who for years had carried a deep sense of shame and low self-esteem. When his father was dying of emphysema the man asked, "Why were we not close to each other?" The father, with perhaps forty-eight hours to live, replied, "Do you remember when you were ten . . . you dropped a toy down the toilet and I had to spend the whole day getting it out?" He went on to recount similar incidents, all trivial. The son left the hospital realizing that his father's only gift was to demonstrate that he was crazy. For almost four decades the son had thought he was unworthy. Only after this death-bed conversation did the son's wounded self-image begin to heal.

Sons also need to watch their father in the world. They need him to show them how to be in the world, how to work, how to bounce back from adversity, how to stand in right relationship to the feminine, outer and inner. They need the activation of their inherent mas-

---

[66] As a therapist I have seldom witnessed more pain than that suffered by a man who never knew his father's love and approval. This wound is most keenly felt by gay men whose fathers, insecure in their own identity, rejected and abandoned their sons.

culinity both by outer modeling and by direct affirmation. Telling a boy not to cry, not to be a sissy, is only to further a life-long self-alienation. Showing him how to be honest in his emotions, how to get up off the floor and back into the fray—the necessary wounding—is what each son needs. He needs to be shown that it is perfectly human to be afraid and, while afraid, that one is still obliged to live one's life and to undertake one's journey.

Sons need to have father tell them what they need to know to live "out there," and how to live with integrity. Sons need to see father living his life, struggling, being emotional, failing and falling, getting up again, being human. When the son does not see his father honestly living his personal journey, then the son will have to find his paradigms elsewhere, or, worse, unconsciously live out the father's untaken journey. This is in accordance with Jung's observation that the greatest burden the child must bear is the unlived life of the parents.[67] On this theme the Rilke poem I quoted in *The Middle Passage* merits repeating here:

> Sometimes a man stands up during supper
> and walks outdoors, and keeps on walking,
> because of a church that stands somewhere in the East.
> And his children say blessings on him as if he were dead.
> And another man, who remains inside his own house,
> stays there, inside the dishes and in the glasses,
> so that his children have to go far out into the world
> toward that same church which he forgot.[68]

The church to which Rilke alludes emphasizes the sacred nature of the journey. (As with Kafka, the Prague-born Rilke would see the "East" as the frontier.) In the one case the father takes his journey, albeit painfully so. In the other, the father stays home, fearful, and his children must overcompensate for what he left undone.

Of course the father's journey need not be a literal departure, but each man must depart in some way from the collective, from security, from his silent mother complex, if he is to become himself.

---

[67] See above, pp. 54-55.
[68] *Selected Poems of Rainer Maria Rilke,* p. 49.

When he does not, in whatever way, blaze his own trail through the dense forest, he becomes part of the psychic entanglement hindering his son's journey.

A father may be physically present, but absent in spirit. His absence may be literal through death, divorce or dysfunction, but more often it is a symbolic absence through silence and the inability to transmit what he also may not have acquired. Dad's defection means that the balance of the parent-child triangle is tipped and the mother-son dyad assumes a disproportionate weight. As well intentioned as most mothers are, they can hardly be expected to initiate their sons into something they are not. Without a father to pull him out of the mother complex, the son stays a boy, trapped either in dependency or compensatory macho suppression of the feminine. His fear and confusion are then liabilities he must mask. The uninitiated male hides his wound, his longing, his grief, a stranger to himself .

It is this longing, this attraction toward the initiating male, that is constellated in the men's movement. Spokesmen such as Robert Bly (looking more like Moses than Charlton Heston), Michael Meade, Sam Keen and James Hillman, quite apart from what they may say, symbolically evoke the wise elders. That Robert Bly's analysis of the fairy tale "Iron John" (or "Iron Hans" in Grimm's original) would become the number one seller on the *New York Times* book list is astonishing, especially since it is not easy to read and employs concepts that are not common currency. But the very fact that its ancient motifs found such a ready response suggests it is a good paradigm for modern men's relationship to the primal masculine.

"Iron John" begins with hunters disappearing in the forest. Psychologically this means that however competent the court, the conscious center of the personality, may seem to be, something is amiss. Energy is being robbed from conscious life. Upon investigation a wild ferric creature is dredged up from a well, the deep, archetypal world. As consciousness is threatened by such obvious power, the creature is immediately caged. But the prince, the youth who represents the potential for growth in the kingdom, drops his golden ball, symbol of his psychic wholeness, into the cage of Iron John.

Iron John tells the boy that if he frees him, he will return the golden ball. But the key to the cage is under his mother's pillow. He must not ask for the key since his mother will not give him that freedom; she does not want her son to become a man who will leave her. The boy does steal the key and unlocks the cage. Iron John carries him off and they undergo a series of symbolic, transformative adventures. The mother's apprehensions were accurate, for her son does leave her; he becomes a man. Of course his actions are not hostile toward her, or the passive king, his father, but necessary initiatory experiences. At the end of the story, the youth no longer needs Iron John's assistance, for he has internalized that strength.

What is so important about this story, as Bly rightly perceived, is that it provides a useful model of male initiation for our time. The boy must leave home psychologically to grow up. The father is no help, for he is also afraid of that archetypal male empowerment. The mother will cling to her child to protect him from the wounding that is necessary to become conscious. Fortunately, the child has access through the archetypal level to the masculine imago within. Like most men today he must bypass the personal father, overthrow the seductive tyranny of his mother complex and seek the activation of his true nature at a deeper level. It is this process that speaks to men in such myths and legends, as well as in modern movies. When the youth does return to the court, after his wounding but subsequently victorious journey in the world, he is able to claim the princess as his outer bride and also the anima within. Comfortable with the primal masculine, he is able to accept the feminine.

Many women have expressed their apprehension of the men's movement and of the Iron John phenomenon in particular. They fear that such talk is a rationale for men to maintain, or regress to, the caveman attitudes that have been so oppressive, and often violent, in the past. But they are confusing, as many men have historically, the task of empowerment with aggression. The man who feels empowered to be himself without shame or apology, without macho bluster or overcompensation, has no need to be hostile and aggressive toward either women or other men. Such a man has nothing more to prove. He has been tested and proved worthy.

Women also have criticized Bly and others for excluding women and for neglecting the father-daughter nexus. The latter charge is true and perhaps in time will be addressed by men, as it has been by some women.[69] For now it seems that men's most pressing task is to learn what they can from each other about the masculine, if and wherever that may be learned. Similarly, women need to learn about being women from wise old women, when and wherever they may be found. Men and women may be more comfortable with each other when they have become comfortable with themselves.

One young man wrote of his experience after a men's retreat:

> I am ancient red, orange and yellow.
> I am animal man, your brother.
> Through the pines and the palms
> I learned how to see
> The dimensions of wonder
> From the great chiefs of peace.
> There's a drumbeat in the forest
> And flutes on the wind.
> I see men joining hands
> As brothers and friends.
> Go drumming my brothers
> Any heartbeat you feel.[70]

Obviously the writer felt something stir deep within, the primal satyr Pan who, like Iron John, incarnates a lost masculine dimension.

Another writer who has contributed to our understanding of the wounding of modern men is Jungian analyst Eugene Monick. In *Phallos: Sacred Image of the Masculine,* Monick points out that the disempowerment of the personal father causes a wound at the archetypal as well as the personal level. Unconscious men who suffer inner doubt, who feel helpless, have created the patriarchy, which oppresses other men, rapes women and despoils nature. Patriarchy,

[69] See, for instance, Linda Leonard, *The Wounded Woman: Healing the Father-Daughter Relationship* and Marion Woodman's books, *Addiction to Perfection, The Pregnant Virgin* and *Leaving My Father's House.*

[70] Timothy Hollis, "Song to Pan." Personal communication.

which has held sway in the West for some three thousand years, is a compensation for inner weakness. Men brandish spears, rockets and skyscrapers when they lack a positive phallic identity. Walk tall and carry a big stick; maybe no one will notice how little you feel. Monick's thesis is a timely reminder that phallos—not to be confused with the penis—is an archetypal force from which derives male potency and largeness of soul.

In *Castration and Male Rage: The Phallic Wound,* a sequel to *Phallos,* Monick argues that men suffer castration because the world wounds their sense of personal identity. The signs of this are over-compensation and an inflated power complex (think of Donald Trump naming his casinos after His Sameness, Wall Street scandals, and the meteoric rise and subsequent fall of business empires), and rage, often directed outward. Men also reveal their disempowerment through timidity and shame. One analysand I met who had been abused by his father could barely hold his head erect and look at me, lest I shame him the same way. Monick too, as I have here, asserts that a primary enemy of men is fear, fear of the feminine and fear of being wounded by other men. Patriarchy, which substitutes power for love and measures worth in material terms, worshipping not the divine but its own erections, is a compensation for this fear.[71]

In *King, Warrior, Magician, Lover: Rediscovering the Archetypes of the Mature Masculine,* Robert Moore and Douglas Gillette recognize the emotional immaturity of the patriarchy on the one hand and on the other seek to make conscious four archetypes of male functioning. Each of these archetypes has a positive and negative side.

The king represents a man's executive function, the power to take control, to make decisions. The shadow side, when the king feels his impotence, is virulent power. He may seek control over others to compensate for his own deficits. His bluster and bravado, power lunches and big cars, are actually symptoms of powerlessness, but he is too terrified to turn within and settle accounts. Thus the king archetype must be consciously owned or a man will be even more

---

[71] See James Wyly, *The Phallic Quest: Priapus and Masculine Inflàtion.*

susceptible to the depredations of the Saturnian patriarchy.

The warrior represents the imperative that a man be prepared to fight for what he desires, for his integrity, for a cause or for justice. The shadow side of the warrior is the destroyer. How much of our history has been drenched in blood by men who, unable to fight for their own truths, or indeed having none, projected their rage onto others and slaughtered them. All wars are civil wars—men against their brothers.

The magician is the archetype of the shape-changer, the protean power of men to move mountains, to adjust to changed conditions, to find a way to make things work. As Sophocles noted twenty-five hundred years ago, "How numberless are the world's wonders / And none more wonderful than man."[72] He who tamed the salt-churned seas, who built roads across the mountains, who wrenched from the recesses of his soul the Fifth Symphony, is the wonder-worker in nature. His shadow side, though, is control, manipulation, sleight of hand and charlatanry. He is not to be trusted. He embodies the ethical edge along which all men walk, the fine line between working wonders and treating the world as a shell game.

The lover, too, walks a fine line—between eros, the force for interconnection, and narcissism, the need for egoistic gratification. Men's hatred is well documented. But, wonderfully, they also love. They love from afar and write the *Commedia;* they love God and write *Ad majoram gloria Dei.* They love their fellow man and write *War and Peace.* They love women and children and sacrifice their flesh and their souls in brute labor to support them. They love their ill brothers and clean and comfort them as they die of AIDS. But they may also deform that eros to terrible ends. Lecturing at the Jung Institute in Zürich in 1978, Paul Walder related an anecdote attributed to the former Swiss ambassador to Berlin. At a state reception in the late 1930s, Hitler reportedly said, "I should have been an architect, but now it's too late."

Each of these archetypes constitutes an energy-filled image. All

---

[72] *Antigone,* in *The Complete Greek Tragedies,* p. 170.

men carry them within; they long for their inner activation and outer manifestation. Alas, the personal father can never activate the full range of archetypal empowerment. Thus men, in their hunger for fathering, suffer their deficits in the recesses of personal shame or seek surrogate fathers in the dubious models so widely available. Clearly, in order to activate true maleness, the images must be drawn from the deep well, down where Iron John lives, and not from the neurotic, overcompensated, self-alienating precincts of patriarchy.

The deep drama of the search for the father transpires daily in every man's life. One reason why Jungian analysts monitor the dream world is in order to track such inner dramas. Often one can measure change by the evolution of certain images or themes through the unfolding dream life. It seems that the psyche is working toward its own healing even when consciousness is not yet ready to assist. By listening to the dream and assimilating its energies, consciousness can grow and facilitate the larger motives of the psyche.[73]

In the last chapter I wrote of the wounding of Allen, an emergency room physician.[74] Allen now knows what he once suspected, that he, the son of two physicians, became one himself primarily to win their approval. His parents always made love conditional and approval dependent on "meeting the program." Three of his dreams, scattered over a twenty-month period, reveal his evolving relationship to the Saturnian father.

In the first dream he is in a room that he knows belongs to his father. The room is dark and oppressive, filled with large antique vases and urns. A young man gives him an old flintlock musket. He takes the musket and fires at the vases, shattering some of them. The dream ends with him feeling "silly, and slightly afraid, like a destructive youngster." Here the psyche places Allen in the confines of the father complex where, indeed, all feels dark and oppressive to him. The room is filled with "old stuff," the debris of childhood. A

---

[73] See, for instance, James A. Hall, *Jungian Dream Interpretation: A Handbook of Theory and Practice,* and Donald Broadribb, *The Dream Story.*
[74] Above, pp. 76-77.

younger part of him, perhaps the rebellious child, perhaps the nascent future, presents him with an old weapon, perhaps the agency of an old anger. He expresses his anger by destroying the containers. Afterward, he feels like an adolescent acting out, self-righteous but slightly embarrassed.

In a dream a few months later Allen sees himself on an island that is under artillery fire. An old man is telling stories of the war and Allen follows him to listen. A shell hits a huge tree that topples on the old man and kills him. Allen knows this tree is called "the soldier tree." The old man had been overbearing and not liked, but he had inspired achievements. Allen feels he might like to die this way also. Then he is among some branches and feels cool rain on his face.

Many of Allen's dreams employed metaphors of warfare. While he had never been in the military, Allen experienced himself as being constantly "under fire," and certainly the emergency room of an inner-city hospital is a kind of war zone. His schedule was frequently four days on and three off, and he always experienced anxiety before returning. By the second day back he had adjusted, which he compared to having been on leave and then returning to the trenches.

In this dream Allen is surrounded by water, by the emotional flood of his life. He is drawn to the old man, a combat veteran from whom he has things to learn. But the man is killed. Allen's reaction is ambivalent. The old man was oppressive and overbearing—but he had also inspired others to achieve. This reflected Allen's ambivalence toward his father. He wanted to love his father, needed to love him, but he knew he had always had to work to win his father's grudging approval. He was also aware that he had accomplished a great deal thanks to his father's expectations. At the same time there is a kind of futility in the dream. He feels he is called to this combat, nothing will avert his fate, and he only hopes he can die a soldier's death as the old man did. The thought offers a degree of comfort and peace as the rain soothes him.

The death of the old man suggests a development in Allen's psyche of which he was not consciously aware—perhaps the death of the old senex values that had governed his life. He feels, as many before him have, doomed to die with his boots on, but the measure of resigned calm may in fact augur a positive psychic shift.

In a third related dream, Allen is once again in a military setting. He has been summoned before the general and has saluted, heard his orders, promised his compliance. But, during the exchange, he is somewhat inappropriately, even defiantly, shining his shoes. As he leaves he salutes again but says to himself, "I am not here for long. I am going over the hill."

Ironically, after his analytic session Allen had been planning to drop by his parent's home for a fourth of July party. The dream, from that same morning, repeats the familiar military metaphor. We know now who the general is in his life, the old man he still outwardly salutes. But it is clear that his rebellion, first seen in the shooting of the vases in the earlier dream, continues. Now his divergence grows greater. Now the psyche announces that changes are imminent. He is saluting for the moment, but sometime soon he will leave it all behind.

Often in therapy one realizes that much of what one did in life, what one became, even the good results, came from the wrong places, from the wounded parts. Allen, for instance, became a physician to win his parents' approval. Such a motive is understandable for a child but not healthy for an independent adult. Yet Allen was a fine, caring physician who may in fact belong in the medical profession. His task was to find out who he was apart from the weight of the parental complexes—what was valid and what was suspect in his professional choice.

Allen's predicament is analogous to that of many men. Some may have had less demanding fathers, some no father at all, but what they share is that they cannot go to their personal father, nor to any wise old men of their tribe, to ask the necessary questions. The "invention" of psychoanalysis a century ago was in response to suffering that could not be alleviated by medicine, by theology or by patriarchal fathers. When men's souls are wounded they respond in ways terrible to themselves and others. They can only change themselves and their society when they become conscious of their wounds.

The father-son wound goes very deep. With the personal father seldom able to help, the son is driven to pseudo-fathers—religious prophets, pop stars, -isms of all kinds. Or he suffers in the privacy of his grieving heart. Few sons can bless their fathers as e.e. cummings does:

> though dull were all we taste as bright,
> bitter all utterly things sweet,
> maggoty minus and dumb death all we inherit,
> all bequeath and nothing quite so least as truth
> —i say though hate were why men breathe—
> because my father lived his soul
> love is the whole and more than all[75]

Cummings is able to bless his father for, in the elder's capacity to live his life fully, he modeled and activated that masculine potential in the son. Such a son is very lucky. For most men, the father, through no fault of his own, is but another in a series of wounded generations. Thus the sons must travel to another place to begin the healing. That place is not where some guru lives or some corporate structure stands; it is in his own skewered and alienated soul.

I am frankly pessimistic about the chances of most men for escaping or transforming a life lived under the shadow of Saturn. Yet, clearly, social change comes about through the awakened consciousness of individuals. When enough reject the values offered them by their culture, values that damage the soul, then social change will occur. Accordingly, it is the task of men everywhere to attain a degree of consciousness that enables them to heal themselves.

And that is the eighth secret men know: *if they are to heal, they must activate within what they did not receive from without.*

That is the subject of our last chapter.

---

[75] "my father moved through dooms of love," in *Norton Anthology of Poetry,* p. 1046.

5

Healing the Souls of Men

Before addressing the issue of healing, a mystery far more profound and elusive than wounding, I think it appropriate to review our material to this point. While it is hardly necessary to rehearse the Saturnian shadow under which we live, the roles, expectations and values that daily injure men, it does seem useful to recall the eight secrets men carry. When I have raised them with men in the context of friendship or therapy, each has acknowledged having such thoughts in his frightened and silent heart. Sometimes a man has been acutely conscious of them since childhood, but often it is our conversation that prompts them to surface out of inchoate emotional confusion.

The Eight Secrets

1) Men's lives are as much governed by restrictive role expectations as are the lives of women.

This assertion requires perhaps the least amplification, for the vast personal and social pathologies of our time are the *cri de coeur* of individual souls deformed by the procrustean roles established by patriarchal thinking. As Rilke observed, "We're not at home, not reliably, in the interpreted world."[76]

We have inherited a world in which a man's prime value is to defend his homeland and provide for his family. These may still be honorable roles, but they are roles at best and not the whole man. He does not have permission to seek and treasure his own soul's calling. He may be successful by the norms of the world, but he knows, deep down, that along the way he has lost his soul. No sane man today really believes that having an attractive wife, a powerful car in the garage and a vacation in the sun is the sum and worth of his life.

---

[76] *Duino Elegies,* p. 27.

But most still serve such superficial values because they know no other. They are then slaves to their work, servants of seductive but evanescent values, and generally adrift in the world our fathers served and that ground them up.

Women have rightly challenged the narrow range of womanhood endorsed by the culture they received. It is equally necessary for men to engage in a radical review of their lives and their relationship to the images and voices that would direct them. Men still carry a large economic burden, for example, but they must increasingly fight for the conditions that enable them to pull the money wagon with dignity and with purpose. And they must increasingly be willing to risk all to save what remains of their soul.

I sometimes imagine an executive at the top of the World Trade Center in New York—lord of his domain, a wife and kids in West-chester, things to do and people to see. But as he watches a boat heading out the Hudson, under the curving lines of the Verrazano Narrows Bridge, his spirits sink. He has achieved all he sought, ful-filled the expectations of his culture, but he knows he is a lost man. As Joseph Campbell expressed it, one can spend one's whole life climbing the ladder, only to realize that it had been placed against the wrong wall.[77]

For men to begin the process of healing they must first risk being honest with themselves, allowing the feelings they think they can't afford. They must admit they are not happy in spite of what they have achieved. They must admit they do not know who they are or what they must do to save themselves. They must overcome the fear that blocks such thinking, the fear that they will have to change their lives if the emotional cat is let out of the bag.

The first step toward healing is perhaps the hardest. Men must stop lying to themselves, and by extension each other, and they must permit their unhappiness to become conscious. They must admit that, perhaps for all the best intentions, their lives are wrong, and that from this point on it is their responsibility to change.

---

[77] *This Business of the Gods . . . ,* p. 19.

2) Men's lives are governed by fear.

All lives are to some extent governed by fear, but men are deeply invested in keeping it at arm's length. Women have the enormous cultural advantage of emotional honesty. Men are afraid of the power of the mother complex and so seek to please women or dominate them. Men are afraid of other men because they are cast into competitive roles; the other man is perceived as an enemy, not a brother. Men are afraid because they know the world is large and dangerous and ultimately unknowable. They feel like children within and the ship they set upon the dark and crashing sea is fragile indeed. Women know this also, of course, but they can admit it to themselves and to other women; their lives are not then so lonely, so isolated, so fraught with self-blame.

Men have the crazy notion that they *ought not* to be afraid, that their task is to conquer nature and themselves. Surely, men have done incredible things, made great leaps into the darkness and returned with marvelous maps of Terra Incognita, but, withal, each man feels shamed by the fear that he is not a real man. His shame manifests as overcompensation when he shows off or bullies others, or in silent avoidance of the real task to which life has called him.

Again, the healing of a man begins the day he can begin to be honest with himself, the day he can acknowledge how much his life is driven by fear, when he can beat back the shame that then threatens to engulf him. Only then can he recover that center which has been obscured by the great gray fear that haunts his soul.

3) The power of the feminine is immense in the psychic economy of men.

The greatest psychological influence in a man's life, under normal circumstances, is his mother. Because of the enormity of this psychic presence, of which he is always more or less unconscious, men develop a distorted relationship to the feminine in four major ways.

First, they grant too much psychological power to women; that is, they project the immensity of their mother complex onto women. Crudely expressed, "You have breasts, you must be a woman. My mother was a woman, you must be like her." So men, fearful of a woman's power, will seek to please or control or avoid confrontation. Unable to recognize and own the issues generated by their mother complex, they fall into a projective relationship based on power. This is the most fundamental truth behind the so-called war between the sexes: fear replaces eros with power.

Secondly, men are terrified of their feminine side. They associate their feeling life, their instincts, their capacity for tenderness and nurturance, with the culturally defined nature of woman and distance themselves accordingly. This also distances them from their own anima and occasions a profound self-alienation. In fact, it may be misleading to speak of a man's "feminine side," for the anima is actually a necessary part of what it means to be a man. Men seldom risk this part of themselves, but it is as much in their nature to relate to the world and to their own inner life as it is in women's.

Thirdly, because men are so insecure in their sexual identity and propped-up gender roles, they fear and deny those parts of themselves that don't fall within narrow collective limits. When they see those aspects being lived out by others, they reject them violently. Homophobia is a prime example. Gay men surely have the right to live according to their sexual orientation. Increasingly it seems that homosexuality is not a choice at all, but a biologically based orientation that has existed in roughly the same percentages throughout history. This genetic spin of the dice is engineered by that same god worshipped by the fundamentalists who supplant love with fear and oppression. Gay men have the same heart, same soul, same courage to go into battle as their heterosexual brothers. It is time to come out of the macho closet and name the real problem—that men fear those who incarnate their unlived life. The enemy is not the other guy, but rather our fear that we are not what patriarchy demands.

Fourthly, men's experience of the power of the feminine has evolved into an overvaluation and fear of sexuality. Nietzsche once observed that the primary purpose of marriage was conversation.[78]

---

[78] "Human, All-Too-Human," in *The Portable Nietzsche,* p. 59.

The purpose of a committed relationship, of which marriage is but one example, is not to take care of each other, to reinforce the parent-child complexes, but to grow through and with each other. Relationship is meant to be dialectical—soulful encounters that temper and enlarge. One of the bridges between the sexes, to be sure, is sex. But men, too often feeling deficient in discourse, place too much emphasis on intercourse.

Whatever sex is, and it is at least a profound mystery, it is easily misused. The primary psychological purpose of sex for those men who spend their lives in the cold, cruel world, and whose relationship with their own anima is frigid, is to reconnect with a warm place. Sex is a form of emotional reassurance, a narcotic to still the pain of the bruised soul. If life batters them, then sex, like drugs or work, may numb the wound. The sexual act offers a momentary transcendence. Orgasm can be an ecstatic experience; for the moment one may feel outside the iron confines of ordinary consciousness. It is the closest many men ever come to a religious experience. Thus the act of sex may mask a desperate search for acceptance, underneath which lurks the mother complex. This is ultimately a destructive game. Sex as loving, sex as conversing, sex as dialectic, all presuppose an equal partner. Sex as redemption distorts the relationship and allows entry to the Saturnian shadow of power. When Saturn is present, nothing is really fun, luminescent or transforming.

4) Men collude in a conspiracy of silence whose aim is to suppress their emotional truth.

Virtually any man will recall occasions when he expressed himself and suffered ridicule or rejection. Men pay a heavy price for being seen to be fragile and vulnerable. They are shamed by other men, sometimes by women, but, most of all, by themselves. Those who daily lay siege to the Castle Perilous need as much self-confidence as they can muster to bolster their shaky hold on a strong self-image. So they collude in keeping quiet about what damages them. The word "conspiracy" derives from Latin *conspirare,* "to breathe together." Men breathe silently together to protect their frightened souls, prolonging the wounding of all.

Again, one comes to the issue of honesty. Individual men must risk speaking the truth, their personal truth, for it will be the truth for many others. An old Chinese saying suggests that the one who speaks the right word will be heard a thousand miles away. For men to stop lying, to stop participating in the conspiracy of silence, they must risk showing their pain. Other men may, reflexively, leap to shame them, or, out of their own fear, dissociate from them. But in time all will come to thank those who speak their truth aloud.

5) Because men must leave Mother, and transcend the mother complex, wounding is necessary.

Having delineated the power of the mother complex, the part of a man that longs for nurturance and safety above all, we must also acknowledge the necessary wounding of the male. Our ancestors, with their rites of separation from childhood dependency to adult independence, were not being gratuitously cruel in wounding their youth. Their wounds were symbolic, hence freighted with archetypal meaning. The wounds were a form of synecdoche, a part illustrating the whole, an introduction to the world's wounding, the experience of which would henceforth become one's daily experience.

When a teammate reminded me that a torn fingernail was the least of the wounds to come, he was being helpful in preparing me for a larger world. When it was third and short yardage, the psyche had to be ready for the necessary collision, to stop the power sweep at the line of scrimmage, not be preoccupied with its own comforts. So the tribal wounding of a youth was a symbolic *rite d'entrée* to the world. But even more, it was a way of helping him to face the coming pain of life and sacrifice his infantile longing for a warm hearth. He was to assume the burden of his journey, its pain and solitude. No one else, parent or tribe, could spare him that journey lest they also steal his capacity to fight for and achieve his full potential.

So men must be wounded to truly enter the world, to have consciousness quickened, to undertake the heroic task of leaving the mother and becoming masters of their own destiny. We are all like

Philoctetes. We feel rejected and hurt; we would like to retire to our separate caves and hang out, full of self-pity. But for each of us the hero task summons: each of us, each day, must struggle anew with the grinning demons of fear and lethargy that confront us from the foot of the bed, eager to eat another piece of our soul.

I never cease to marvel at the capacity of men (and women too, of course) to leave home and venture into the unknown. I never cease to admire the courage of those who first crossed the mountains, who navigated the wine-dark seas, who went down into Hades' kingdom and wrote "Sonnets to Orpheus" or the Fifth Symphony. And I ask myself, as Yeats did, "Why should we honor those that die upon the field of battle, a man may show as reckless a courage in entering into the abyss of himself."[79]

Beyond wounding lies a new level of consciousness. If we were to live without the wounds that, like a psychopomp, lead us into the unknown, without the strange and wonderful adventures along the way and the blood-burnished trophies with which we return, would life be worth anything? The price we pay for greater consciousness, and worlds worth winning, is the wounding of the protagonist so that he might become the hero in his own life.

6) Men's lives are violent because their souls have been violated.

The wounds men suffer today are not symbolic; that is, they do not transform. Because our culture lacks meaningful rites of passage, images that would activate and direct the energies of the soul, most modern men feel weighted, even crushed, by their roles and the expectations, outer and inner, upon them. Nothing helpful is touched and moved. Whatever wounds can also destroy. Violate a man's soul and some part of him becomes violent. Mass-murderers and serial killers have all suffered violent verbal and physical abuse. The frustrated postal employee or bank clerk who goes berserk has become commonplace on the six o'clock news. But that is only the tip of the iceberg. Soul murders occur all the time in the lives of men.

---

[79] Richard Ellman, *Yeats: The Man and the Masks,* p. 6.

Not only are men called upon to do the dangerous, dirty, difficult job, to hang from the bridge and scrape the paint flecks, to push back the physical and psychological barriers of nature, to hold up under pounding pressures, to stay cool and collected, they are also expected to suffer such wounding in silence and solitude. Most of all, they are asked, as women too have often been asked, to sacrifice their soul to serve some economic, political or cultural norm. They are shamed if they resist the deformation of their nature, shunned if they protest, and sometimes even martyred if their vision too strongly challenges the status quo.

Men need to acknowledge their anger, anger that has accumulated to the level of rage. Where does that rage go? For some it manifests as depression, a general heaviness they may carry their whole life long. For others it somatizes in sundry provinces of the body or is projected in the paranoid game of us and them, winners and losers. For many the rage is acted out against women and children or other men, the deep knowledge of their soul's suffering projected onto any convenient object.

There has been enough brutality in the world to last forever. Now men must channel their anger to fuel the changes imperative to healing. We cannot help but suffer passively when we are children; we cannot help but be victims while we remain unconscious. But once we become conscious we are responsible for our lives. The anger that has grown through the years is now energy enough for change, for rebellion, for the necessary struggle to save the soul.

7) Each man carries a deep longing for his father and for his tribal fathers.

As great as is the inner pressure, the deep pull back and down into the realm of the Mother, so must a corresponding force emerge to bridge the psyche over the great-in-between. This was the wisdom embodied in tribal rites of passage out of childhood. The rites were extensive, psychologically powerful, and prolonged to the degree that the mother complex had power over the nascent ego.

To leave the comforts of home, the mother world, one must have some place to go. Admittedly, the rites of passage of traditional cultures were to initiate the youth into a simpler society, a more homogenous culture than ours. As well, their interest lay not in the individuation of the person but in the integration of that unformed person into the collective definition of tribal masculinity. Still, take away such psychically charged images of identity, take away the wisdom of the elders, take away the community of men, and one has the modern world.

Since nature abhors a vacuum, so men today, childlike and uninitiated, fill the great-in-between with drugs, work, their partners. If we learn relationship by relating to the otherness of others, we confirm our identity by modeling like to like. Men today cannot claim their identity via the culture because they are obliged to find other uninitiated males as their models or succumb to the empty values of a materialist society. Again, before healing may begin, men must acknowledge the reality of what lies within. Among those confusing emotions is a deep grief for the loss of the personal father as companion, model and support, and a deep hunger for the fathers as a source of wisdom, solace and inspiration.

It was the office of the tribal elders to pass on the wisdom of the ancestors, to inform the youth of the gods whom he was to serve and who stood by him. Men today have no rooting in any tribal history or transcendent reality. Men who have no grounding connection with their gods are in grave peril and they will bring danger to others as well. Such men are lost. They feel abandoned by history and the wise old men. They long for modeling and for the great teachings. They suffer their exile in silence or act out their grief disguised as rage. Such men are legion.

8) If men are to heal, they must activate within what they did not receive from without.

Because men cannot turn to tribal elders, and have learned there are few if any wise men, let alone initiated ones, they suffer a deep sickness of the soul. Since the psychic loci, the mythological points of reference, are missing, men must learn to heal themselves. Occasionally, such healing may be shared with their fellows, but, by and large, they must go it alone.

In his novel *Demian,* Herman Hesse, who certainly addressed the healing of the modern soul, suffering exile and persecution thrice and the Nobel Prize once as recompense, observed, "In a world of wanderers, when paths intersect, the world feels like home for awhile."[80] But the experience of community, of primal connection, is only for "awhile"; then one is back on the journey alone.

The Mother Complex / Father Task

A review of the morphology of the mother complex is warranted here. Again, the formative power of the personal mother in the psyche of the child is enormous. The child's experience of the mother is internalized as a complex, an emotionally charged cluster of energy beyond the control of the ego. As the mother is the bridge to the world of nature and the body, and to relationship, so the boy's experience of her ripples through his archetypal depths.

In other words, a man's relationship to himself, to others and to the life force that courses through him is profoundly channeled by his primary experience of mother. To the extent that she is unable to meet his needs, and imposes her personal complexes on him, so he will suffer the wounds of abandonment and overwhelment. From the former he learns to distrust his own worth and the reliability of the world. Because of the latter he feels powerless to defend his fragile frontier and so evolves a generally compliant, co-dependent personality or a fearful, overcompensated, power-dominated one. In either case, he is not himself, but lives in reaction to an experience so powerful that it subordinates his natural truth. This compromise formation, repeated throughout childhood, produces a false personality and furthers the projection of that first relationship onto later, adult relationships. Thus he lives a false self.[81]

---

[80] *Demian,* p. 104.

[81] See *The Middle Passage,* chapter 1, for further discussion of the collision between the false, acquired personality and the natural self.

Since the child is completely dependent, any threat to his neediness occasions great fear. All men carry within them the replicated memory of this vulnerability. They suffer enormous fear that their needs may not be met, fear that their neediness will prolong their dependency. Out of this troubled condition, which remains with men however old, are bred anger and sorrow. Men are angry that their needs are not met and they grieve the loss. As they grow older and are battered and buffeted by the roles of adulthood, these emotions tend to slip into the unconscious. But such energies do not go away; they go somewhere, always. Their anger may be deeply introverted as a life-long depression, or somatized in emotion that attacks the body. They may act out by beating women and bashing gays, or, more abstractly, by corporate head-butting. Their anima, which they suspect because it reminds them of the mother world, is kept at bay. She, naturally, expresses herself in irritability and general bitchiness. The man's sorrow manifests as melancholy, as addictions whereby he slips fuzzily into the mother, or through a vague longing for a beloved who will enter his life and heal him.

Beneath all of these dynamics are, on the one hand, men's fear that they will not be taken care of, and, on the other, an overwhelming terror of dependency. Thus men fight the feminine, both within and without, as a result of their largely unconscious fear of their own incestuous longing for peace.

Since all men carry the mother imago deep within, charged variously from one to the other, so the result of their restricted consciousness is to produce a highly defended and narrow definition of the masculine. Men evolved the patriarchy, with its rules, hierarchical thinking and social structures, and its subjugation of the feminine, as a defense against the mother complex. Fathers and sons can barely talk to each other, lest they be obliged to share the shameful secret that the fathers are castrated and seek to castrate their sons, even as Cronus-Saturn did. The compensation, then, is just as killing as the problem it seeks to defend against. Both the fearful suppression of the complex and the patriarchal reaction alienate men from themselves.

Men everywhere are fated to face their partners, institutions or some emotional analogue, carrying the dynamics of childhood as a contemporaneous experience. The past is not truly past. Mother and father live within, every moment—not only the personal parents, but the collective experience of them as well. Thus, feeling all the old need, the old fear, the old longing, the old anger, albeit unconsciously, men project these dynamics onto the current Other. That Other, then, has the power the primal parent once had, which men will variously try to control or placate, or even avoid altogether.

This explains why so many men seem angry and controlling at home and in the workplace. It also explains why there seems to be an increase in those who may be described as passive-aggressive. They feel powerless, but they are angry and will find a way to sabotage or subvert the Other. Their powerlessness is all the more acute as there are so few positive models of masculine empowerment that show how to tackle such large needs and fears oneself, thereby lifting their projections off others.

Men can never be in reality, that is, deal with the Other as genuinely different, if they cannot discern the effect of their mother complex rippling within. Yes, it takes a great deal of courage, insight and patience, as well as steady work, to make such material conscious. It is especially difficult for men to work with the mother complex, since uncovering its power and influence in their lives tends to jeopardize the frail hold they already have on their masculine identity. But, until men can take the risk, they will remain stuck in a compensated identity that only furthers their inner division and their estrangement from others.

What Is Healing, and Who the Healer?

Before we can realistically address the healing of men, we must first examine what healing means and where in our time healing agencies may be found.

Franz Kafka wrote a prophetic story at the beginning of this century titled "The Country Doctor." A physician is called out in the middle of a raging snow storm to attend a patient. When he arrives the villagers are all crowded around a young man. The youth says to the physician, "Save me, save me." The doctor examines his patient and proclaims that he can find nothing wrong; no apparent wound or diseased condition. Again, "Save me, same me," the youth cries. The doctor looks again and sees a gaping sore in the patient's side, with multiple rose-red layers. Worms as thick and as long as his finger wriggle to the light. After a further examination, the doctor explains that he cannot save him. The villagers are incensed and engage in a ritual divesting the doctor of his powers. They chant, circle him, strip off his vestments and throw him out into the wild. Struggling to find his way back through the darkness, the physician thinks:

> That is what people are like in my district. Always expecting the impossible from the doctor. They have lost their ancient beliefs; the parson sits at home and unravels his vestments, one after another; but the doctor is supposed to be omnipotent with his merciful surgeon's hand. Well, as it pleases them.[82]

Kafka's story has metaphoric and prophetic meaning. The power of the clergy has waned, supplanted by a new superstition and a new priest, in a white coat instead of black. But the new religion, medical science, cannot save either. Only upon closer examination does the symbolic rose-red wound become visible. Science, with all its marvelous powers, is powerless to heal such a wound. Thus the physician becomes another dismantled servant of a discredited divinity. Kafka warns us against placing our faith precisely where the twentieth century has placed it—in the external, quantifiable world. Our wounds are to the soul, and only that which reaches it can heal.

The physician is a servant of *Physis* (nature). The physician does not heal; nature heals. (From Latin we get *medicus,* "healer," *mederi,* "to heal" and *docere,* "to lead.") When the body is broken the physician may promote conditions that facilitate healing, but cannot heal wounds to the soul. Decades ago D. H. Lawrence realized this:

> I am not a mechanism, an assembly of various sections.
> And it is not because the mechanism is working wrongly,

---

[82] *The Penal Colony,* p. 141.

that I am ill.
I am ill because of wounds to the soul, to the deep
    emotional self
and the wounds to the soul take a long, long time,
    only time can help
and patience, and a certain difficult repentance,
long, difficult repentance, realisation of life's mistake,
    and the freeing of oneself
from the endless repetition of the mistake
which mankind at large has chosen to sanctify.[83]

Our society has long treated men as machines, as bodies expendable in the name of progress or profit. Men have overruled their pain and soul's delight, taught to think of themselves as "mechanisms." Such an estrangement wounds very deeply; it has gone on so long and is so taken for granted that healing individuals, let alone a whole gender, is a dubious undertaking. But the beat goes on, the Saturnian shadow lives, the only game in town, and shame on the defector. The wounding is institutionalized and sanctified, and men unwittingly collude in their own crucifixion.

All men suffer from neurosis. The word itself suggests a mechanical failure and, indeed, derives from the Enlightenment's effort to create models of the cosmos and models of men. But in fact neurosis simply signifies the deep split between socialization and soul, between collective culture and individual psyche. When outer roles do not fit the shape of one's soul, a terrible one-sidedness occurs. It is the suffering of this imbalance that impels men to war on themselves and on each other.

The role of the therapist is to attend this split and to observe what images emerge, be they cognitive, of the body or of dream-life. Such images are symptoms. The German word for symptom, *Zustandsbild*, means "picture of a condition," representing the psyche's effort to heal itself through a symbolic bridging. Symptoms partake of both the unconscious depths and the conscious world. They bridge as

---

[83] "Healing," in Robert Bly, James Hillman and Michael Meade, eds., *The Rag and Bone Shop of the Heart*, p. 113.

metaphoric agents. The word "metaphor" is from Greek *meta,* "over, across," + *pherein,* "to carry." Thus psychotherapy is etymologically akin to waiting upon or attending the expression of soul. Jungian analysis is not reductive but synthetic; the word "analysis," from the Greek *analusis,* does not mean to rationalize but "to undo, loosen." Images that undo or loosen one's conscious perception of oneself are the basis for the process by which the psyche heals itself. In Jung's words:

> The mediatory product [e.g., image or symbol] . . . forms the raw material for a process not of dissolution but of construction, in which thesis and antithesis both play their part. In this way it becomes a new content that governs the whole attitude, putting an end to the division and forcing the energy of the opposites into a common channel. The standstill is overcome and life can flow on with renewed power towards new goals.[84]

Healing the soul is a process not unlike that of creativity itself, so perhaps the work of the artist is a useful paradigm. The artist is engaged by images that float upward into consciousness. Many artists have testified that they might start out with an idea for a work, but then something else takes over. Their best work, they claim, comes when they are able to surrender their ego and their talent to express those images in paint, sound or words. Thus, as Jung noted, the creative process involves the "activation of archetypal images and the shaping of those images into the finished work."[85]

Depth psychotherapy activates nascent images in the psyche and then supports a dialogue with them. Jung described this process as the transcendent function, by which the Self seeks to transcend the barriers between consciousness and the unconscious. In other words, the psyche seeks to heal itself. This approach to healing is therefore homeopathic rather than allopathic: like cures like. Healing comes from resonance, the re-sounding or re-cognition of likeness. Men's healing comes when the proper images are modeled by their fathers or the tribal elders, or when they themselves can activate

---

[84] "Definitions," *Psychological Types,* CW 6, par. 827.
[85] Ibid.

those images. Personal healing, soul healing, comes through the evocation of symbolic images or acts that resonate and mediate the split.

Shamanic healing in traditional cultures frequently employed the recitation of creation myths, foundation legends of the tribe, for in those narratives lay images that evoked the transcendent function in the psyche of the suffering patient. When such images were deeply accepted and consciously integrated, healing was possible. Today analysts assist this process by attendance, by fidelity and by collaborating with the images. But always, whenever healing occurs, it is due to a transpersonal, mysterious agency, experienced as grace. Then, as Rilke reminds us, we "know that there is room in us / for a second large and timeless life."[86]

Seven Steps to Healing

In this last section I will advance seven concepts that support the possibility of healing. None of them is original, but together they may promote a move in the right direction, both for individuals and for men collectively.

Let me repeat that while I respect those participating in the current men's movement, I do not expect such efforts will achieve much. Already aspects of the movement seem faddish and passé, perhaps unfairly so, but clearly its strength is fading. I believe that collective change will occur only when enough individual men change. From the work of self-healing, to whatever level we can bring it, the focus of our culture will change.

This may be a forlorn hope, but it is more realistic than to expect sudden shifts in collective consciousness. I expect men will continue to feel the pressure of traditional Saturnian dictates. They will still be called to sacrifice their bodies and their souls for economic ends. They will still be expected to collude in the silence that supports patriarchal values and estranges them from other men and from themselves. And they will still carry their grief and rage to early graves.

---

[86] *Selected Poems of Rainer Maria Rilke,* p. 19.

But my hope, at least, is that individual men will become conscious, saving themselves and helping others. Perhaps some will even become the wise elders we all need.

Here, then, are seven steps toward self-healing, followed by a discussion of each.

1) Re-member the loss of the fathers.

2) Tell the secrets.

3) Seek mentors and mentor others.

4) Risk loving men.

5) Heal thyself.

6) Recover your soul's journey.

7) Join the revolution.

1) Re-member the loss of the fathers.

If we are to learn our nature from those of our own gender, then our relationship to both our personal and tribal fathers is critical. But ever since the Industrial Revolution and the vast urban migration— which is to say, for the past two centuries—most men have lost their roots: their relationship to their homes, to the work of their hands, and to their souls. In return for greater economic security they have adapted their energies to roles that serve profit but deform the soul.

Such men have suffered grievous wounds and, in their pain and unknowing, have wounded their sons. Like the tragic curse in a Greek drama, the wounds ripple through the generations. Only men who make such an historic wounding conscious, who see it in their lineage and re-member themselves, that is, heal the split, may transcend the Saturnian weight of history. Few have more dramatically rendered the experience of living with a wounded father than Sharon Olds in her appropriately titled poem "Saturn."[87]

> He lay on the couch night after night,
> mouth open, the darkness of the room
> filling his mouth, and no one knew
> my father was eating his children.

---

[87] In Bly et al., *Rag and Bone Shop of the Heart,* p. 128.

She goes on to describe how her father eats each child in turn. She believes that

> in the nerves of his gums and
> bowels he knew what he was doing and he could not
> stop himself.
> . . . .
> This is what he wanted,
> to take that life into his mouth
> and show what a man could do—show his son
> what a man's life was.

Other sons saw their fathers suffering the Saturnian burden, just as I saw my father leave the assembly line to shovel coal on weekends into the bins of others. How much we took for granted—food on the table, the rent paid, shoes to wear. In "Those Winter Sundays," Robert Hayden remembers his father's struggles and his own innocence and indifference. With pain in his heart he recalls

> Speaking indifferently to him,
> who had driven out the cold
> and polished my good shoes as well.
> What did I know, what did I know
> of love's austere and lonely offices?[88]

These were our fathers, more wounded than we can imagine, with no alternatives or emotional permission to be themselves, and unspeakably lonely. For such men we must unashamedly grieve.

Grief is honest. It values what was lost, or was never there. Men carry this heaviness in any case, most often as a depression they may not even be aware of. Depression is a blunting of the life force; however deeply we may press the father loss into the unconscious, the psyche knows and condemns us to carry that weighted feeling. Grief is open remembering, and while it may not feel very good at the moment, it is cleansing and healing in its honesty. Depression may involuntarily pull us under, however functional our outer life. Even life's sweetest moments may be tinged with this heaviness.

---

[88] Ibid., p. 142.

One man, a stock broker, drove himself as his father had once driven him. He could not relax. Weekends were the time to catch up on his work. His father had only valued work, so, to win his father's approval, he worked himself to the edge. Even though the father was dead, the father imago remained charged and drove him still. Even when he exceeded his father's financial status he could not let up. After two years of therapy he managed to stop working on weekends and, finally, visit his father's grave for the first time. There he wept for the tenderness and acceptance that he would never receive from his father. His tears, his grief, allowed him to begin moving forward in his own life, a life he scarcely knew at all, having been defined previously by the Saturnian shadow of the wounded and wounding father.

If grief pushed underground produces depression, so does anger denied. Anger is a legitimate and reflexive reaction of the organism to wounding. Once I had an analysand who casually announced he had involved his sons in incestuous acts. They had collaborated, he averred. I felt my anger rise for the boys who were looking for father's love and for father's touch and found one who would betray their powerlessness, their naivete and unconscious literalism, mistaking bodily sex for love. I asked him to speak about this to his now adult sons and be willing to suffer their grief and their anger. The hope was that they might heal somewhat, even if he would not.

The anger many sons feel gnaws at them, in their ulcers, their migraines, their drivenness to achieve the affirmation every child deserves. Men need to get angry at the wounds, as well as the wounder, if they are ever to heal. One may well ask what good that does so long after the fact. But anger, like any powerful emotion, does not go away. It always goes somewhere. The wounded son will wound *his* son if he does not cleanse himself and break the cycle. If anger may clear the air and produce a fresh beginning with the still-living father, then it must be risked. If anger will drive the wedge only deeper, then it must be a conscious decision not to confront. But each son must confront that anger within himself or he stays the prisoner of Saturn.

It is imperative that men render what is inside of them more conscious. They certainly cannot change the past, nor, often, can they change the outer father-son relationship. But what they do not know operates silently within them nonetheless. Given Jung's profound observation that the greatest burden the child must bear is the unlived life of the parent, so each father's son must examine, without the motive to judge, where his father's wounds were passed on to him. Either he finds himself repeating his father's patterns or living in reaction to them—in both cases he is Saturn's prisoner.

Each father's son must ask himself, "What were my father's wounds? What were his sacrifices, if any, for me and others? What were his hopes, his dreams? Did he live out his dreams? Did he have emotional permission to live his life? Did he live his life or the Saturnian tapes? What did he receive from his father and culture that hindered his journey? What would I have liked to know from him about his life, his history? What would I have liked to know from him about being a man? Was he able to answer such questions, however tentatively, for himself? Did he ever ask them? What was my father's unlived life, and am I living it out, somehow, for him?"

These are the mostly unspoken questions between generations. If they are not voiced consciously, their implicit answers have been lived out unconsciously, often in wounding ways. When we ask such questions, even of a deceased father, we are more likely to avoid idealizing or devaluing him. He becomes more a man like us, a brother who has suffered the same ordeal. Then we are more likely, even in the case of severe wounding, to operate out of compassion. If we are caught up in hate we stay bound to that which wounds us. When we understand our fathers better, from the vantage point of adults, we are better able to begin the process of fathering ourselves.

2) Tell the secrets.

Those in the healing professions know that wherever there is denial the wound festers. Or, as the twelve-step programs put it, what one resists, persists. Men's lives are based on denial and resistance to the truth. Rarely does one hear the unvarnished truth, as in the confession of Pablo Neruda: "It so happens I am sick of being a man."[89] Note that he does not say he is sick of being himself; it is his role as a man that sickens him. This is the deepest truth men carry, that their souls are deformed through being defined by outside forces. For every Thoreau who slips away to the woods for awhile to find his soul again, to engage in a radical revisioning of his life, there are a million men, and women too, who every day slide back into collective anonymity and soullessness. They lead, in Thoreau's memorable phrase, lives of quiet desperation.

Since the psyche knows more than consciousness, this deformation of soul is recorded and occasions a concatenation of responses. The most notable of reactions is the tinge of sorrow that haunts men's lives even though they may cover themselves well. Again, Neruda tells the truth, inescapably:

> There are expanses,
> sunken factories, pieces of timber
> which I alone know,
> because I am sad, and because I travel,
> and I know the earth, and I am sad.[90]

The other tell-tale sign is their rage which, misdirected and undifferentiated, turns on themselves and others. And underneath all this "fury and mire of human veins"[91] is the terrible fear. No man feels he is a real man. His macho behavior belies his terror. W.H. Auden also told the truth:

> Patriots? Little boys,
> obsessed by Bigness,
> Big Pricks, Big Money, Big Bangs.[92]

When men sense that they are frauds, that is, caught between their soul's intention and external demands, they are forced to dissimulation. Estranged progressively from their inner life, their anima, they

---

89 "Walking Around," in ibid., p. 105.
90 "Melancholy Inside Families," in ibid., p. 104.
91 W.B. Yeats, "Byzantium," in *The Collected Poems of W.B. Yeats,* p. 243.
92 "Marginalia," in *The Collected Poems of W.H. Auden,* p. 592.

expect women to carry the burden. Sex, in particular, is given too much importance, for through it men seek to overcome their isolation from their feeling state and from their own body. They ask the Other to reconnect them and to reassure them before the dawn brings new battering. This makes them as vulnerable and dependent as before. As humans must hate those upon whom they depend, so tension and animosity grow, and eros is replaced by the shadow of power.

These are the central secrets of men—that they feel themselves failures as men, that is as persons who happen to be men, that they are torn between fear and rage, and that they are emotionally dependent but resentful of the object of that dependence. Again, the only way out is consciously to acknowledge these insufferable truths. They must begin with themselves and then share that truth with others—not with a woman but with another man. That man, caught also in fearful defendedness, may scorn the truth-teller, his scorn in proportion to his fear, but he may also step from behind the ramparts to acknowledge his brother.

Our mythology is full of heroic adventures—mountains climbed, ogres fought, dragons defeated—but it takes even more courage for a man to speak his emotional truths. The hero quest today is not through the physical world but through the badlands of the soul. The evil men must engage is not the barbarian at the gates but the darkness within, the fear from which only boldness may bring delivery. Jung described this heroic task:

> The spirit of evil is fear, negation, the adversary who opposes life in its struggle for eternal duration and thwarts every great deed, who infuses into the body the poison of weakness and age through the treacherous bite of the serpent; he is the spirit of regression, who threatens us with bondage to the mother and with dissolution and extinction in the unconscious. For the hero, fear is a challenge and a task, because only boldness can deliver from fear. And if the risk is not taken, the meaning of life is somehow violated.[93]

Our fear is the task—failing the task we bluster into macho compensation or shamed complicity. Telling the truth of our soul to our-

---

[93] *Symbols of Transformation,* par. 551.

selves is the first task. Living that truth is the second task. And telling it to others is the third. Such truth-telling will be the supreme test of our lives. Afterward, perhaps, we can stop being "sick of being a man."

3) Seek mentors and mentor others.

As mentioned here earlier, when I began my practice about fifteen years ago, the ratio of women to men who sought therapy was perhaps nine to one. Today, without seeking to change my clientele, the ratio is about six to four in favor of men. This shift tells me several things: that men are in deep trouble, that many know it, and that the climate of the collective has shifted somewhat and therapy is therefore less risky.

In fact it is men of greater emotional strength and core honesty who seek therapy. The others are too fearful. Some, like the man dragged into therapy by his wife, who condescended toward the box of tissue at his elbow and the cauterizing tears they implied, are in the deepest trouble. They are at war with their partners and themselves.

Therapy offers a unique opportunity for men to share their lives privately, to be emotionally honest and know they are not going to be shamed, to share secrets about the task of being a man. For awhile, the enormous ring of isolation is lifted. For many men therapy also serves as a rite of passage, a separation from the mother and initiation into the male world. They often come in, as men generally do, thinking their issue is "out there," that if they can "fix the problem" their lives will get back on track. In time they come to realize that their whole life is wrong, that choices made unconsciously led them down labyrinthine paths of ever-greater self-estrangement. They may realize they have a troubled relationship to the feminine, but they seldom suspect that She is in them. They have an enormous longing for the fathers though this is fundamentally unconscious. And they often come to recognize that they have lost their gods, their connection to nature and their own body.

Generally, for all the pain they feel, these men are often curiously numb. But they feel even more pain as they become conscious. They realize they need the teaching of the wise elders and they long for greater meaning in their lives. They also learn that they must heal themselves; their partners cannot. Then they cry and rage, and admit the fear. When these things happen, healing begins.

Most men will not enter therapy of course. They lack the means and opportunity, or are too afraid of the huge emptiness they might find inside. Yet even they may turn to other men and pass on what they have learned, or learn, from others. A mentor is one who has visited the other side and can tell us something of what it's like there. Collectively, men have a lot to share. As individuals they are frightfully separated. The men's groups dotting the continent are truly wonderful opportunities for sharing and mentoring, but most men will never go near them and will suffer their isolation forever.

Unfortunately, few mentors are to be found. How many men have had an initiatory experience and integrated that experience into a working Weltanschauung? Boys still need that older man to teach and model the knowledge of the outer world. But who, as Nietzsche asked, will teach the teachers? Who will initiate the mentors? The truth, once again, is that in our time there is no collective rite of passage, no mythically grounded body of experience to assist men in their journey. So, they must do it as individuals. And such individuals, like the bodhisattvas of Buddhism, can reach back and, out of simple compassion, bring their fellows along.

4) Risk loving men.

Recently an analysand observed how necessary but how difficult it was for him to risk loving men. As a particularly insightful, and courageous man, he acknowledged that the problem was his own homophobia, literally, fear of men. Why should he be afraid of men, his own gender after all?

Yes, we have all grown suspicious of each other, for we have been conditioned to be competitive. We are ever wary, fearful that the other fellow might get the upper hand, the old patriarchal power game. But in considering this dilemma we have to take it deeper than a social wounding and find the source of homophobia truly within.

Just as men have commonly narrowed their relationship to women through the fragile bridge of sexuality, so men are afraid to love each other lest they sexualize that relationship. Even gay men may be homophobic, for they have even more to fear from their fellows. Thus, again, the silent hand of fear plays a determining role.

Physical camaraderie is permissible on the playing field. Men may hug, slap and hold each other, even weep together, in the locker room. Men may share even their blood in combat. Recently a female analysand went white-water rafting in Canada. The river was perilous and her life was in jeopardy, but she fought through her fear, learned to control her boat and had a wondrous bonding experience with her male boatmate. After a few days, she said, they thought as one and did not have to talk to know how to navigate the rapids. I told her she had had a very rare experience, one that men, if they ever have it, treasure all their lives.

There are few things more rewarding than for a shortstop, deep in the hole, to turn and throw the ball toward second, and see the second baseman intersect base and ball at the exact moment. This is less about practice than about the integration of spirit, the communion of soul. Perhaps this rare sense of oneness is possible in part because the outer challenge occasions a transcendence of the individual ego to serve the joint purpose, but perhaps also because the occasion allows men to feel their masculine natures without threat or ambiguity. In less animate, less transcendent, settings, the old doubt and ambiguity insinuate themselves anew.

How sad, that men have so few transcendent meetings outside of sports and warfare. How rare, to have an emotionally intimate male friend. Intimacy between men is largely superficial compared to that between women. Most men would sooner die than discuss their fears, their impotence, their fragile hopes. They ask women to carry that emotional burden. As mentioned in the first chapter, I was constrained from sharing my feelings with a men's group leader in Santa Fe, though we surely had a lot to talk about. But I have a friend in Indianapolis and one near Vienna with whom I can pick up the paragraph we left unfinished years before. And as a therapist I have been privileged to have some wonderful moments with men, conversations that could only occur as I grew more and more comfortable with myself, less fearful, more willing to disclose.

Like the paradox of Jesus, that one can only love the neighbor to the degree one can love oneself, so men can only learn to love other men if they can learn to love themselves. Our self-blame and rage are projected onto other men, whom we then avoid. When we acknowledge that we are estranged from our brother because we fear him, and that we fear him because we are riddled with fear of ourselves, then we have taken the first step toward love. The opposite of love is not hatred; it is fear. The most difficult part of loving other men, as individuals or as a group, is that we have to take the terrible risk of loving ourselves. Such self-acceptance in the face of failure and fear is profoundly difficult. But replacing homophobia with eros and caritas begins at home.

5) Heal thyself.

Repeatedly the point has been made here that the tribal elders are missing in action. And we know that healing occurs from like to like, re-sonance, re-cognition, re-membering. So wounded men wound their sons and other men. The cycle of Saturnian sacrifice finds ever new youth to grind up. If there is any gospel, or good news, in this book, it is that nonetheless healing can and does occur.

We cannot change our culture and its impact on us. And we certainly cannot change our personal history with the huge influence of parents, living and dead, or how we internalized that history and our cultural context, adapted ourselves to it in order to survive. Almost all of us, then, lost our way along the road. Longing for mentors, the blind lead the blind.

In *The Middle Passage* I presented many examples of how we develop a provisional personality in reaction to childhood experience, how we set off into life with this false self and make choices that further estrange us, and how by midlife we suffer the growing split between the acquired personality and the natural self. All men, at whatever stage of life, need to traverse this middle passage and save their lives. The first passage, of course, is leaving home physically, not knowing one is carrying inner baggage in accord with which one will later make inauthentic choices. The final passage brings aging and confrontation with mortality.

A good illustration of the dues that must be paid by a man who has not found himself along the way is dramatized in Tolstoy's "The Death of Ivan Ilyich." The name Ivan Ilyich would translate roughly as "John Johnson," so we know we are dealing with an Everyman motif.

Ivan lives his life unconsciously, accepting socially prescribed roles. Then he is stricken with a mortal illness and finds he has no inner reality to turn to. His wife and friends are similarly empty and of no help. He finally concludes, as one in therapy often does, that his whole life has been a sham, someone else's sense of what his life was about rather than his. Then he has to confront the greatest fear all men carry, not the fear of death but the fear that he had not truly lived his life. His middle passage, the move from a provisional, childhood-bound, culture-driven life, to authentic manhood had not occurred and he was as woefully unready to meet death as he had inadequately lived life. The crux of the middle passage is the requirement that a man, whatever his age or station, pull out of his reflexive behaviors and attitudes, radically reexamine his life, and risk living out the thunderous imperatives of his soul.

Once having identified the role mother plays in our development, the subsequent mother complex with its archetypal reverberations, and the loss of the father and the absent elders, we know something of what we must face on our own.

Men carry their psychological history within, especially the longing of the child for nurturance and protection. That child is subsequently flung out into the world to fight and ultimately die. Because the enormous longing for a safe harbor persists, men have generally landed women with this burden. But most women rightly resist mothering the man in their life, so men must take on this role. Robert Bly recounts the Australian aborigine rite of passage for boys. The men sit in a circle and cut their forearms and press the blood into a bowl. Then, in a communion of blood, they pass the bowl and drink from it, older man and youth alike, saying, "Mother's milk nourished you. Now father's blood nourishes you."[94]

Men understandably fear being dependent, but they should not fear their need for nurturance. All creatures need care and feeding. The male overcompensation for dependency—the lonely drifter on the plains, the John Wayne, Clint Eastwood model—is pathological, as anyone who has to live around such a person will testify. Men must accept their need for nurturance. And whether they seek it from women or other men, they need to recognize that the care and feeding of themselves is primarily their own responsibility. Then fear of and need for others is put into proper perspective.

If nurturance is the archetypal need behind the boy's relationship to his mother, so we might say that empowerment is the archetypal need that seeks fulfillment from the father world. He needs to see father develop a relationship to his own inner truth, deal with fear and shame, hold the feminine in respectful balance, and go about the business of building a new world out there. Personal empowerment is not to be confused with the power complex. The power game castrates all men. Empowerment means that one feels good energy available for the tasks of life. One feels the permission to dive into life and struggle for depth and meaning. One feels that there are resources within to draw upon when the forces of darkness are nigh. Again, it would be helpful to have the model of the personal father at close hand to activate such empowerment, but most men will have to do it on their own.

In effect, the mother and father complexes are charged clusters of energy having a life of their own beyond the control of consciousness. Each man must inventory his own internalized imagos and discern what their message is regarding the capacity of life to sustain itself and the power to fight for still greater life. How are those clusters charged? With what messages, implicit and explicit? Where have they led to false choices?

---

[94] *Iron John,* p. 121.

The same sort of questions asked above in an effort to understand and grieve the father must be asked by each man of himself. What are his own wounds and aspirations, his unlived life? Each man must ask anew the questions he wanted his father to ask for him. If he wanted to know how to be a man, how to cope with fear, how to find courage, how to make unpopular choices, how to balance masculine and feminine energies, how to locate and move in accord with the soul's gyroscope, he must now risk those questions to himself. And if he does not know the answer he is at least asking the right questions. As Rilke once wrote to a young friend:

> Be patient toward all that is unsolved in your heart and try to love the *questions* themselves. . . . Do not now seek the answers, which cannot be given you because you would not be able to live them. And the point is, to live everything. *Live* the questions now. Perhaps then you will gradually, without noticing it, live along some distant day into the answer.[95]

A man must ask himself, for example, what fears block me? What tasks do I, in my heart of hearts, know I must undertake? What is my life calling me to do? Can I bring my work and my soul closer together? How can I serve both relationship and individuation? What areas of father's unlived life must I occupy and plant my own flag on? Then comes the moment of decisive significance, the risk, the boldness to live the questions in the existential world. Being a man means knowing what you want and then mobilizing the inner resources to achieve it. This may seem simplistic, but it is not. For a start, it is extraordinarily difficult to know what one wants. How does one separate the inner truth from the cacophony of personal complexes and cultural directives? And how, having discerned one's truth, does one summon the courage to live it in the real world?

It is this kind of questioning and daring, in outer and inner worlds, that makes a man. The past and the Saturnian weight of culture play powerful roles, but the psyche is resourceful and will supplant the past with insurgent energies to forge a different future. Jung

---

[95] *Letters to a Young Poet*, p. 35.

once observed that we do not solve our problems, we outgrow them.[96] This capacity of the psyche to enlarge is what makes healing possible. We all would still like mother to take us in her arms and nurture us, and we long to stand behind father while he leads the way. But that is not going to happen. Each man must shed the directives of the parent complexes and make his own decisions, feed his own hungers. What was not activated by the parents, or was activated only in partial ways, must now be self-activated.

I recall a man who as a child had lost his father in World War Two. For years he had grieved his loss, always feeling inadequate and unprotected in a hostile universe. He would often attach himself to powerful or learned men, even occasionally to ideologies, in search of the missing father strength and wisdom. One week, while vacationing by himself in Cape May, he held a series of dialogues with his dead father, asking all the questions he had never had a chance to. He felt a presence within himself, one with whom he conversed and who did in fact respond to his questions.

Of course he was not talking with his actual father, but with the father imago, a part of his own nature that he himself, by his questions, had activated. The personal father is not there to be imitated in a slavish fashion; he is needed to activate by example and by affirmation the father imago in the son. When the father is absent, or too wounded to serve the purpose, the son is left with the deficit. This can be significantly, if not totally, overcome by the son, by turning his questions, fears and aspirations inward and respecting the images that come. Through active imagination and dreams, the son can be in touch with the empowering father after all.

The biological parents are charged with a large responsibility for transmitting and activating the life force in their child, much more than they can reasonably achieve, given their own wounding. But the son can, through courage and deep soul-work, surpass the limitations imposed by his parent's wounds. This work he does not only

---

[96] "Commentary on 'The Secret of the Golden Flower,'" *Alchemical Studies,* CW 17, par. 17.

for himself but for his children and for the world in which he lives. As Nikos Kazantzakis proposed the task:

> Humanity is such a lump of mud, each one of us is a lump of mud. What is our duty? To struggle so that a small flower may blossom from the dunghill of our flesh and mind.[97]

The scarab beetle, known for its habit of rolling dung-balls, was sacred to the Egyptians, for they saw, ineluctably, that something living could come out of the dung. So too may one rescue a wounded soul from the dross of personal history.

6) Recover the soul's journey.

Men are now free to make their first secret known—that their lives are as restricted by role definitions as are women's—thanks to the courage of women who have protested at traditional roles and institutions that deny uniqueness and equality. Women have led the way. Predictably, many men have resisted the effort of women to free themselves because men not only felt something would be taken away from them but, even more, they thought they were comfortable in their rigidly defined gender roles. That their roles were oppressive and deforming did not occur to most men until women forced them to look more closely.

The average man still is reluctant to examine his life lest he be obliged to change, and change always occasions anxiety. But when one realizes that the anxiety accompanying change is preferable to the depression and rage occasioned by constriction, change becomes more attractive. Jung noted that neurosis is the necessary outcome when the infinite possibilities of the individual are subordinated to the restrictions of the culture:

> I have frequently seen people become neurotic when they content themselves with inadequate or wrong answers to the questions of life. They seek position, marriage, reputation, outward success or money, and remain unhappy and neurotic even when they have attained what they were seeking. Such people are usually confined

---

[97] *The Saviors of God,* p. 109.

within too narrow a spiritual horizon. Their life has not sufficient content, sufficient meaning. If they are enabled to develop into more spacious personalities, the neurosis generally disappears.[98]

Jung's list of false goals and golden idols matches the Western dream of success, yet men do not feel successful even when they have achieved those goals and sacrificed to those idols. They feel uneasy, shamed and alienated. Who can forget the family standing around the grave of Willy Loman in Arthur Miller's *Death of a Salesman?* While his friend Charley offers the eulogy for a working man driven to ground by tough times, Willy's son speaks the sad truth: "Charley, the man didn't know who he was."[99]

Surely there is no sadder epitaph for a man, especially one who has worked hard and been broken. Why else are we here, on this still spinning planet, if not to try to know ourselves? Men have stopped asking the right questions and so suffer a sickness unto death. They can only save themselves by recovering a sense of their soul's journey. They have to do this; they really have no choice.

Recently an analysand brought the following dream:

> I am with a man in water. He has a bad leg. He goes under. I should help him but I am not a good swimmer. I have to do something. I am afraid, but I dive under and find him on the bottom and pull him up. I give him CPR. I had to do it. No one else would do it. He comes to and breathes.

That drowning man is the dreamer himself, which ego-consciousness intuits and knows it must rescue. He may only save and be saved when he is willing to take the dive into his own depths and administer the life-giving re-spiration *(spiritus)*. No one can do it for us; we must renew the hero journey of old and dive into our depths. This is the proper work of man, the work that saves.

After the inner work men will be able to take a necessary look at their outer world. Most men use their job to validate themselves, but they do not feel valued even when they have achieved success. They

---

[98] *Memories, Dreams, Reflections,* p. 140.
[99] *Death of a Salesman,* p. 138.

use work to validate their identity when they have not done the work of individuation. As Albert Camus noted, "Without work all life goes rotten. But when work is soulless, life stifles and dies."[100] While we cannot ignore economic realities, we must also ensure that our work give meaning and substance to our lives. It is necessary for men to decide anew, then, who they are and how they will spend their precious energy.

No man may leave home or be in the world without suffering grievous wounds to body and soul. But he must learn to say, "I am not my wound or my defense against my wound. I am my journey." The wounds of life may crush the soul or they may quicken consciousness. But only ever-greater consciousness can bring luminosity to the journey. Miguel de Unamuno sounds the challenge:

> Shake off this sadness, and recover your spirit. . . .
> Throw yourself like seed as you walk, and . . .
> don't turn your face for that would be to turn it to death,
> and do not let the past weigh down your motion.
>
> Leave what's alive in the furrow, what's dead in yourself,
> for life does not move in the same way as a group of clouds,
> from your work you will be able one day to gather yourself.[101]

The recovery of the soul's journey is necessary for man to save himself. He must again be able to see himself in a larger context, in the framework of the eternal. Jung asks of a man what we must all ask of ourselves:

> Is he related to something infinite or not? That is the telling question of his life. . . . If we understand and feel that here in this life we already have a link with the infinite, desires and attitudes change. In the final analysis, we count for something only because of the essential we embody, and if we do not embody that, life is wasted.[102]

It does not matter whether a man feels at home in some religious or political or domestic form. He *is* his journey, and that is what is of

---

[100] *Resistance, Rebellion, and Death,* p. 96.
[101] "Throw Yourself Like Seed," in Bly et al., *Rag and Bone Shop of the Heart,* p. 234.
[102] *Memories, Dreams, Reflections,* p. 325.

decisive significance. The terror he may feel on the high seas of life is understandable, but in relinquishing the imperative to sail on, in giving over to an ideology or to dependency on someone else, he loses his manhood. It is time to come clean, acknowledge the fear, but live the journey.

The summons to journey is not a justification for narcissism. A man still is obliged to fulfill his commitments to others, to meet his responsibilities. Yet he has an inescapable calling to individuation. If he forgets that calling, squanders his brief moment on earth, he is a problem to those others anyhow. To live the journey of the soul is to serve nature, to serve others and to serve that mystery of which we are the experiment. Then we will have incarnated the invisible, made luminous this short episode between two great mysteries.[103]

7) Join the revolution.

If this book seems pessimistic about imminent social change and somewhat skeptical about men's movements, it is yet optimistic about the power of individuals to gain consciousness, to find the courage to change, to reclaim their lives—and thereby bring about change in the world.

Historically, change occurs when a culture has become too one-sided. The compensation exists, then, in the unconscious of all its citizens. It takes a person of intuitive gifts, that is, one to whom unconscious material is more readily available, to bring those neglected values to the surface. The artist, perhaps, is the one who first incarnates the neglected value in a work ahead of its time. He may suffer ridicule or rejection or, worse, indifference, but his seed begins to germinate in the liminal zone of others. The prophet may be martyred, but his truth has already challenged the collective. And just so now, the cat is out of the bag, the Saturnian cinctures loosened. Change is in the air. No wonder dictators suppress artists and visionaries, for they are most dangerous to the Saturnian control that group-think requires.

---

[103] Jung: "Life . . . is a short episode between two great mysteries, which yet are one." *(Letters,* vol. 1, p. 483)

In the nineteenth century children were property to be sold or leased to others. Women were chattel without rights or respect. And from the beginnings of history men have oppressed each other as well. If the rights of children now have a place in our sensibility, and if women are demanding, and deserving of, respect, so men have to become more than soulless machines. The French General Lyautey was admonished, as he set out to plant a certain sapling, that the tree would take a hundred years to reach full maturity. "Why, then we must begin this very afternoon," he replied.[104] So, we too must begin this very day. Each of us is part of the problem, or, individually, part of the solution. Until all are free, none are.

It is time to stop the lies: time to oppose those who say that one is a man when he has power over another man, or a woman, or a child. It is time to oppose all who would oppress others—fearful bigots, unctuous politicians and the like—and, most of all, time to oppose the tyrannous silence that perpetuates Saturn's rule, shaming and separating men. Let the secrets of men be told. They are the Lilliputian threads that will bind the giant.

To join the revolution does not oblige one to stand on a soapbox. It means that one starts to be honest about one's own life. The revolution begins at home, with oneself. Now the reader knows that he is not as strange as he might have feared, that he is not really alone, that other men have experienced what he has, and that they are suffering with him side by side.

The revolution begins when men stop deceiving themselves, when they acknowledge and take responsibility for their secrets. They will still have to struggle and suffer, but they may now be honest. They have to start at home, with themselves, and realize that the Saturnian assumptions with which they have grown up castrate and destroy them as surely as the tyrant gods of old with their severing sickles.

The man who walks out from under Saturn's shadow in his personal life is also doing a great thing for others, whether they know it or not. He has learned that no one has power over him if he does not

---

[104] *The Little, Brown Book of Anecdotes*, p. 372.

give it to them. He has recovered the worth of his own soul's journey. His life takes on a new meaning and his prayer, in the words of Kazantzakis, "is the report of a soldier to his general: This is what I did today, this is how I fought to save the entire battle in my own sector, these are the obstacles I found, this how I plan to fight tomorrow."[105] When this man, and that man, and the other one over there, begin to take personal responsibility for their lives, the old tyrants will lose their grip.

It is said that Zeus heard rumors about a power in the universe greater than power itself, and he was deathly afraid. In the usual manner of a bully, Zeus, with his henchmen Force and Might, swaggered about and intimidated others. Even Prometheus, whose name suggests that revolutionary foreknowledge, suffered on the rock in the Caucasus. But that energy could not be suppressed forever. It is the force all bullies and tyrants fear—it is Justice, before whose bar even the gods must tremble.

When the tyrant gods are overthrown, when individuals walk out from under the shadow of Saturn, when they reject collective expectations and seek their own path, then justice returns. Yes, currently most men are still oppressed; acting out of their own hurt, they oppress other men and hurt women and children. Surely, justice is a long way off. But each of us is obliged to find it, first in our hearts and then on the long road ahead.

> Traveller, you have come a long way led by that star.
> But the kingdom of the wish is at the other end of the night.
> May you fare well, *companero;* let us journey together joyfully
> Living on catastrophe, eating the pure light.[106]

---

[105] *The Saviors of God,* p. 107.
[106] Thomas McGrath, "Epitaph," in Bly et al., *Rag and Bone Shop of the Heart,* p. 256.

Bibliography

Agee, James. *A Death in the Family*. New York: Bantam, 1969.

Alighieri, Dante. *The Comedy of Dante Alighieri*. Trans. Dorothy Sayers. New York: Basic Books, 1963.

Auden, W.H. *The Dyer's Hand*. New York: Random House, 1962.

_____. *The Collected Poems of W.H. Auden*. New York: Random House, 1976.

Bly, Robert. *Iron John: A Book About Men*. Reading, Mass.: Addison-Wesley Publishing Company, 1990.

Bly, Robert; Hillman, James; and Meade, Michael, eds. *The Rag and Bone Shop of the Heart*. New York: HarperCollins, 1992.

Broadribb, Donald. *The Dream Story*. Toronto: Inner City Books, 1990.

Campbell, Joseph. *The Masks of God: Creative Mythology*. New York: Penguin Books, 1964.

_____. *The Masks of God: Primitive Mythology*. New York: Penguin Books, 1969.

_____. *This Business of the Gods . . .* In Conversation with Fraser Boa. Toronto: Windrose Films, 1989.

Camus, Albert. *Resistance, Rebellion, and Death*. New York: Alfred Knopf, 1961.

Clothier, Peter. "Hammering Out Magic." In *Art News*, November 1991.

Complete Greek Tragedies, The. Trans. David Green and Richard Latimore. Chicago: University of Chicago Press, 1960.

Corneau, Guy. *Absent Fathers, Lost Sons: The Search for Masculine Identity*. Boston: Shambhala Publications, 1991.

Crowell's Handbook of Classical Literature. Ed. Lilian Feder. New York: Thomas Crowell, 1964.

cummings, e.e. *Poems 1923-1954*. New York: Harcourt, Brace and Co., 1954.

Dunn, Stephen. *Not Dancing*. Pittsburgh: Carnegie-Mellon University Press, 1984.

Eliade, Mircea. *Rites and Symbols of Initiation*. New York: Harper, 1958.

Eliot, T.S. *The Complete Poems and Plays.* New York: Harcourt, Brace, 1962.

Ellman, Richard. *Yeats: The Man and the Masks.* New York: Dutton, 1948.

Fuller, Simon, ed. *The Poetry of War, 1914-1989.* London: BBC Books and Longman Group UK Limited, 1989.

Gardner, Robert L. *The Rainbow Serpent: Bridge to Consciousness.* Toronto: Inner City Books, 1990.

Grimm Brothers. *The Complete Fairy Tales.* New York: Pantheon, 1972.

Gurdjieff. *Meetings with Remarkable Men.* New York: Dutton, 1963.

Hall, James A. *Jungian Dream Interpretation: A Handbook of Theory and Practice.* Toronto: Inner City Books, 1983.

Hamilton, Edith. *Mythology.* New York: Mentor, 1969.

Hawthorne, Nathaniel. *The Portable Hawthorne.* New York: Viking, 1960.

Hesse, Herman. *Demian.* New York: Bantam, 1965.

Hillman, James, and Venturi, Michael. *We've Had a Hundred Years of Psychotherapy and the World Is Getting Worse.* San Francisco: Harper Collins, 1993.

Hollis, James. *The Middle Passage: From Misery to Meaning in Midlife.* Toronto: Inner City Books, 1993.

Hopcke, Robert. *Men's Dreams, Men's Healing.* Boston: Shambhala Publications, 1989.

Hopkins, Gerard Manley. *The Poems of Gerard Manley Hopkins.* New York: Oxford University Press, 1970.

Johnson, Robert A. *He: Understanding Male Psychology.* New York: Harper and Row, 1977.

Jones, Ernest. *The Life and Work of Sigmund Freud,* vol. 1. New York: Basic Books, 1953.

Joyce, James. *The Portable James Joyce.* New York: Bantam, 1982.

Jung, C.G. *The Collected Works* (Bollingen Series XX). 20 vols. Trans. R.F.C. Hull. Ed. H. Read, M. Fordham, G. Adler, Wm. McGuire. Princeton: Princeton University Press, 1953-1979.

_____. *Memories, Dreams, Reflections.* Ed. Aniela Jaffé. New York: Random House, 1963.

Kafka, Franz. *The Penal Colony: Stories and Short Pieces.* Trans. Willa and Edwin Muir. New York: Schocken Books, Inc., 1961.

Kazantzakis, Nikos. *The Saviors of God.* Trans. Kimon Friar. New York: Simon and Schuster, 1960.

Kierkegaard, Soren. *The Journals of Kierkegaard.* New York: Harper, 1959.

Kipnis, Aaron. *Knights without Armor.* Los Angeles: Jeremy Tarcher, 1991.

Lee, John. *At My Father's Wedding.* New York: Bantam, 1991.

Leonard, Linda. *The Wounded Woman: Healing the Father-Daughter Relationship.* Boston: Shambhala Publications, 1983.

Little, Brown Book of Anecdotes, The. Ed. Clifton Fadiman. Boston: Little, Brown, 1985.

Maloney, Mercedes, and Maloney, Anne. *The Hand That Rocks the Cradle.* Englewood Cliffs, NJ: Prentice-Hall, 1985.

McCracken, Harold. *George Catlin and the Old Frontier.* New York: Bonanza Books, 1959.

Miller, Arthur. *Death of a Salesman.* New York, Penguin, 1976.

Modern Poems: An Introduction to Poetry. Ed. Richard Ellman. New York: Norton, 1973.

Modern Verse in English. Ed. David Cecil and Alan Tate. New York: MacMillan, 1958.

Monick, Eugene. *Castration and Male Rage: The Phallic Wound.* Toronto: Inner City Books, 1991.

_____. *Phallos: Sacred Image of the Masculine.* Toronto: Inner City Books, 1987.

Moore, Robert, and Gillette, Douglas. *King, Warrior, Magician, Lover: Rediscovering the Archetypes of the Mature Masculine.* San Francisco: Harper, 1991.

Nietzsche, Friedrich. *The Portable Nietzsche.* Trans. Walter Kaufmann. New York: Viking, 1986.

Norton Anthology of Poetry. Ed. A. Alison. New York: Norton, 1970.

Osherson, Sam. *Finding Our Fathers.* New York: Free Press, 1986.

Pederson, Loren. *Dark Hearts: The Unconscious Forces That Shape Men's Lives.* Boston: Shabhala Publications, 1991.

Perera, Sylvia Brinton. *Descent to the Goddess: A Way of Initiation for Women.* Toronto: Inner City Books, 1981.

Ressler, Robert, and Schactman, Tom. *Whoever Fights Monsters.* New York: St. Martin's Press, 1992.

Rilke, Rainer Maria. *Duino Elegies.* Trans. David Oswald. Einsiedeln, Switzerland: Daimon Verlag, 1992.

_____. *Letters to a Young Poet.* Trans. M.D. Herter Norton. New York: W.W. Norton and Co., 1962.

_____. *Selected Poems of Rainer Maria Rilke.* Trans. Robert Bly. New York: Harper and Row, 1981.

Schwartz, Delmore. *The World Is a Wedding.* New York: New Directions Press, 1948.

Shakespeare, William. *The Complete Works of Shakespeare.* Glenview, IL: Scott-Foresman, 1970.

Sharp, Daryl. *The Secret Raven: Conflict and Transformation.* Toronto: Inner City Books, 1980.

_____. *The Survival Papers: Anatomy of a Midlife Crisis.* Toronto: Inner City Books, 1988.

Thomas, Dylan. *Collected Poems.* New York: New Directions Publishing Co., 1946.

Thoreau, Henry. *The Best of Walden and Civil Disobedience.* New York: Scholastic Books, 1969.

von Franz, Marie-Louise. *Puer Aeternus: A Psychological Study of the Adult Struggle with the Paradise of Childhood.* 2nd ed. Boston: Sigo Press, 1981.

Woodman, Marion. *Addiction to Perfection: The Still Unravished Bride.* Toronto: Inner City Books, 1982.

_____. *Leaving My Father's House: A Journey to Conscious Femininity.* Boston: Shambhala Publications, 1992.

_____. *The Pregnant Virgin: A Process of Transformation.* Toronto: Inner City Books, 1985

Wyly, James. *The Phallic Quest: Priapus and Masculine Inflation.* Toronto: Inner City Books, 1989.

Yeats, William Butler. *The Collected Poems of W.B. Yeats.* New York: MacMillan, 1963.

Index

140

Studies in Jungian Psychology
by Jungian Analysts

Quality Paperbacks

Prices and payment in $US (in Canada, $Cdn)

Phallos: Sacred Image of the Masculine
Eugene Monick ISBN 0-919123-26-0. 30 illustrations. 144 pp. $16

The Survival Papers: Anatomy of a Midlife Crisis
Daryl Sharp ISBN 0-919123-34-1. 160 pp. $15

The Middle Passage: From Misery to Meaning in Midlife
James Hollis ISBN 0-919123-60-0. 128 pp. $15

Castration and Male Rage: The Phallic Wound
Eugene Monick ISBN 0-919123-51-1. 144 pp. $16

Getting To Know You: The Inside Out of Relationship
Daryl Sharp ISBN 0-919123-56-2. 128 pp. $15

Eros and Pathos: Shades of Love and Suffering
Aldo Carotenuto ISBN 0-919123-39-2. 144 pp. $16

Descent to the Goddess: A Way of Initiation for Women
Sylvia Brinton Perera ISBN 0-919123-05-8. 112 pp. $15

Addiction to Perfection: The Still Unravished Bride
Marion Woodman ISBN 0-919123-11-2. Illustrated. 208 pp. $18pb/$20hc

The Creation of Consciousness: Jung's Myth for Modern Man
Edward F. Edinger ISBN 0-919123-13-9. Illustrated. 128 pp. $15

The Illness That We Are: A Jungian Critique of Christianity
John P. Dourley ISBN 0-919123-16-3. 128 pp. $15

The Pregnant Virgin: A Process of Psychological Transformation
Marion Woodman ISBN 0-919123-20-1. Illustrated. 208 pp. $18pb/$20hc

The Jungian Experience: Analysis and Individuation
James A. Hall, M.D. ISBN 0-919123-25-2. 176 pp. $18

The Phallic Quest: Priapus and Masculine Inflation
James Wyly ISBN 0-919123-37-6. 30 illustrations. 128 pp. $16

Personality Types: Jung's Model of Typology
Daryl Sharp ISBN 0-919123-30-9. Diagrams. 128 pp. $15

The Sacred Prostitute: Eternal Aspect of the Feminine
Nancy Qualls-Corbett ISBN 0-919123-31-7. Illustrated. 176 pp. $18

The Cassandra Complex: Living with Disbelief
Laurie Layton Schapira ISBN 0-919123-35-X. Illustrated. 160 pp. $16

Close Relationships: Family, Friendship, Marriage
Eleanor Bertine ISBN 0-919123-46-5. 160 pp. $16

Chicken Little: The Inside Story (A Jungian Romance)
Daryl Sharp ISBN 0-919123-62-7. 128 pp. $15

Add Postage/Handling: 1-2 books, $2; 3-4 books, $4; 5-8 books, $7

Write or phone for complete Catalogue of over 60 titles

INNER CITY BOOKS, Box 1271, Station Q
Toronto, ON, Canada M4T 2P4   **(416) 927-0355**